THE WAR IN NORTH
AFRICA, 1940–1943

THE WAR IN NORTH AFRICA, 1940–1943

A Selected Bibliography

Colin F. Baxter

Bibliographies of Battles and Leaders, Number 16
Myron J. Smith, Jr., Series Adviser

Greenwood Press
Westport, Connecticut • London

Library of Congress Cataloging-in-Publication Data

Baxter, Colin F.
   The war in North Africa, 1940–1943 : a selected bibliography / by
Colin F. Baxter.
      p.   cm.—(Bibliographies of battles and leaders, ISSN
1056–7410 ; no. 16)
   Includes index.
   ISBN 0–313–29120–9 (alk. paper)
   1. World War, 1939–1945—Campaigns—Africa, North—Bibliography.
I. Title. II. Series.
Z6207.W8B36 1996
[D766.82]
016.94054′23—dc20   95–39494

British Library Cataloguing in Publication Data is available.

Library of Congress Catalog Card Number: 95–39494
ISBN: 0–313–29120–9
ISSN: 1056–7410

First published in 1996

Greenwood Press, 88 Post Road West, Westport, CT 06881
An imprint of Greenwood Publishing Group, Inc.

Printed in the United States of America

∞™

The paper used in this book complies with the
Permanent Paper Standard issued by the National
Information Standards Organization (Z39.48–1984).

10 9 8 7 6 5 4 3

Contents

Contents vii

Series Foreword

The Greeks at Thermopylae, the Crusades, the Armada campaign, Trafalgar, Verdun, Gettysburg, El Alamein, Pork Chop Hill, Khe Sahn, the Falklands, and "Desert Storm" are only a few of the many campaigns and battles, large and small, which have been fought down through the ages. Of course, each of these operations had leaders ranging in quality from Leonidas at Thermopylae to the group think of Vietnam and all featured diverse strategy, tactics, and weaponry. It appears to be mankind's unhappy lot that war has been and apparently will for sometime continue to be a growth industry, despite centuries of horror-filled record-keeping and preventative lessons available for the learning. With only a few exceptions, monographic bibliographies of individual battles and leaders (our series title admittedly, is borrowed from the famous American Civil War history), campaigns and weapons have not been compiled previously. Contributors to this series while thus breaking new ground have also constructed works suitable for wide general audiences. These tools may profitably be employed at every level from high school through graduate university and by the casual researcher/buff as well as the dedicated scholar.

Each volume begins with a narrative overview of the topic designed to place its subject within the context of specific wars, societies, and times; this introduction evaluates the significance of the leader, battle, or technology under study. Each work points to key archival and document collections as well as printed primary and secondary sources. Citations are numbered, allowing easy access via the index(es). Individual volumes may present discussion of their citations in styles ranging from bibliographical essays to individually annotated entries and some titles provide chronologies and suitable appendix(es).

It is my hope as editor that these bibliographies of battles and leaders will enable broad audiences to select and work with the best items available within literature and to benefit from the wisdom of some of today's leading military scholars.

Myron J. Smith, Jr., Series Adviser
Tusculum College
Greeneville, Tennessee

Preface

This book, a volume in the Bibliographies of Battles and Leaders series, is intended to be a reference and research guide for the student, scholar, and general reader with an interest in the War in North Africa, 1940-43.

Part I is the heart of this historiographical bibliography. Each chapter will discuss and evaluate what has been written on that particular topic, while at the same time identifying the main issues and controversies that have been raised about the War in North Africa and the personalities who fought in the desert. My aim has been to integrate the enormous literature consisting of books, articles, memoirs, and other sources that relate to the War in North Africa into a complete tapestry, thus making the battles and personalities understandable from a broad perspective. The final chapter includes some observations and suggestions for future research on the War in North Africa.

Part II of the book consists of an extensive, but selective, alphabetical listing of the leading and significant contributions to the writing on this controversial campaign. Citations are cross-referenced from the historiographical narrative in Part I to the alphabetical listing in Part II and vice versa. The Index includes only those sources discussed at some length in Part I of the text.

I would like to extend a special thanks to the following individuals for their suggestions, encouragement, and assistance in the writing of this bibliography: Correlli Barnett, Norfolk, England; Carlo D'Este, New Seabury, Massachusetts; Eugene Rasor, Emory & Henry College; David R. Woodward, Marshall University; Myron J. Smith, Jr., series editor; Beth Hogan, Inter-library librarian, ETSU; Dr. Richard Sommers, David Keough, and James Slonaker, U.S. Army Military History Institute; Jane Yates, The Citadel; Moira MacKay, University of Manchester; and my friends and colleagues, Professors W. Douglas Burgess Jr., Ronnie M. Day and Stephen G. Fritz. Finally, I would like to acknowledge the support, encouragement and patience of my wife, Tamara, and son Andrew, without whose help this book would not have been written.

Part I

NARRATIVE AND HISTORIOGRAPHICAL SURVEY

1

Historical Background

"What in the world are we doing in the desert? Who would fight over sand?" Such are the questions young American soldiers asked themselves in the desert wastes of North Africa in 1943. Unlike the Hollywood image of golden sand dunes and Palm trees, the North African desert where Allied and Axis soldiers fought between 1940 and 1943 was more like the featureless landscape of the moon. A surface of grit, stones, and rock instead of golden sand covered much of the landscape. The scorching heat of summer, sometimes reaching 110 degrees in the shade, and the hot desert wind or *khamsin*, turned the grit into choking clouds of dust, while in winter, heavy rains formed the dust into bottomless mud.

Who fought in the deserts and djebels (hills) of North Africa? Italians, British, Germans, Americans, Australians, Indians, New Zealanders, South Africans, Poles, Greeks, and soldiers of every color made up the Allied and Axis armies. The diversity of the British and Allied forces was reflected in the forty languages that were spoken by their troops.

The combat that see-sawed back and forth across the desert during the first phase of the War in North Africa occurred in a strip of territory only 40 miles wide at the most, that extended for 1,200 miles between Tripoli in the west and Alexandria in the east---only small ports like Tobruk and Benghazi in between were of any military value because of the critical need to supply armies with everything from water and food to tanks and the fuel without which they were useless. The German commander of the 21st Panzer Division General Johann von Ravenstein would say, "This warfare is a paradise to the tactician, but a nightmare to the quartermaster."[296]

Fighting in the desert, or "The Blue" as veterans called it, resembled war at sea; with practically no roads and few landmarks, men moved by compass. The Australian war correspondent Alan Moorehead in his classic work, *African Trilogy* [339], a brilliant eyewitness record of a world at war, observed that "One did not occupy the desert any more than one occupied the sea." With no trenches and no front lines, mobile forces sought not the conquest of territory or positions, but combat with the enemy. "We hunted men, not land," wrote Moorehead, "as a warship will hunt another warship." Both Axis and Allied writers describe the desert fighting as chivalrous--- quarter was asked and given. If desert wells were sometimes poisoned by retreating troops, and remembering too that the mine is scarcely a chivalrous weapon, it can still be said that war in the desert was as, Rommel termed it *Krieg ohne Hass*, or War without Hate.

If terrible thirst, flies, and danger were the common lot of friend and foe alike in the North African desert, the rival armies could engage in combat knowing that few civilians would be killed in the fighting. Except for the small ports along the Mediterranean, most of the two thousand mile long battlefield was virtually empty desert. Urban settlement consisted of small ports along the Mediterranean. The population was sparse, poor, and semi-nomadic. The desert people of North Africa, however, would suffer for decades after the war from the twenty million mines left behind in the ground by the belligerents.

The war was not all death and discomfort. In his foreword to Wolf Heckmann's book, *Rommel's War in Africa* [204] General Sir John Hackett recalled his days as a young soldier in an armored unit; the desert climate was healthy and bracing, remembered Hackett, and the young men living in it felt physically fit and well. The grim and somber were present, but most young men recalled Hackett, particularly in the early days found it enjoyable---"It was all interesting, too, and exciting, and the company was very good." "Most of us really *liked* being there," wrote Hackett.

What was so important about North Africa that three years of fighting were conducted across its hot barren wastes? In his book, *Brute Force: Allied Strategy and Tactics in the Second World War* [145], author John Ellis doubts whether "the whole campaign barely merits an extended footnote," when compared to the titanic campaign in Russia. Ellis proceeds, however, to give three reasons why North Africa merits more attention than a quick head-count of divisions engaged might indicate. First, the Luftwaffe's involvement was considerable. From May 1942 to June 1943, almost 20 per cent of Luftwaffe combat strength was deployed in the Mediterranean, and in 1943 one-third of all German aircraft losses were sustained there. Second, the German divisions that continued to be tied down in the Mediterranean theater after 1943 were lost to other theaters, most especially to Normandy in 1944 where they might have intervened against the Allies with distrastrous effect. Third, it was in North Africa that the Allied forces learned their trade. In reply to critics who dismissed the War in North Africa as a mere sideshow, a secondary theater of minor importance when compared to the Russo-German war, French Admiral Raymond DeBelot declared in his study, *The Struggle for the Mediterranean, 1939-1945* [128], that "Even if final victory was not gained in the Mediterranean final defeat was here avoided." DeBelot asserted that the early battles were no less important that the later ones, and were fought with less strength and often with inferior weapons. The question of whether an Axis advance to the Middle East in 1941 or 1942 could have won the war is still one of the most controversial in the history of World War II.

Once famous names in the early period of the War in North Africa, such as Field Marshal Sir Archibald Wavell, General Richard O'Connor and Field Marshal Claude Auchinleck, have largely faded into distant memory. Similarly, epic sagas of the desert fighting like Tobruk, where Australian troops were besieged for eight months, and the island of Malta that for two years withstood relentless enemy air attack, and the Allied convoys that sustained the island, are receeding into a distant, yet treasured, past. The name Rommel, the famous "Desert Fox," is far from forgotten, however. His boldness as an armored commander in the desert war is widely recognized even if opinions differ widely on other aspects of his life and generalship. Mussolini described him as merely "a good battalion commander," whereas biographer David Irving, in his book, *On the Trail of the Fox* [233], called Rommel "a twentieth-century Hannibal."

The most controversial military commander of the War in North Africa (and in World War II) was the dynamic little man in the black beret--- "Monty." As the American war correspondent John Gunther remarked, "When you mention Monty to people, they may curse or grin." Historians have been equally divided in their assessments of Field Marshal Bernard L. Montgomery who became world-famous as a result of defeating Rommel at the Battle of El Alamein.

So too did the name General Dwight D. Eisenhower who commanded the first Anglo-American amphibious landing in World War II. A new phase of the war in North Africa opened on November 8, 1942, when American troops together with British forces landed in French North Africa as part of Operation *Torch*. In the subsequent Tunisian campaign, Generals George S. Patton, Jr., and Omar Bradley were among the American commanders who began their rise to fame in North Africa. The cold, the mud, and the rain of that long wet Tunisian winter of 1942-43 would long be remembered by the soldiers, as would place names like Hill 609 (Djebel Tahent), scene of an epic battle by the U.S. 34th Division, and "Long Stop" Hill (Djebel El Almara), the fortress-like position that guarded the road to Tunis where the British 78th Division battled to gain its heights. The Tunisian campaign was a bitterly fought contest, one of grinding toil and demoralizing casualties, in which rifle companies were reduced to platoon strength. From Kasserine Pass to Bizerta, wrote Bradley in *A General's Life* [54], "In Africa we learned to crawl, to walk---then run." When Tunis finally fell on May 13, 1943, and 275,000 German and Italian soldiers passed into Allied captivity, the three-year long War in North Africa had at last come to an end.

Gallons of ink have been spilt on the often bitter controversies and arguments surrounding the battles and leaders involved in the war in North Africa. Each general has had his champion, and detractor. In memoirs, histories, and revisionist accounts it has been argued that victories could have been even more complete, achieved at less cost, or even avoided altogether. The War in North Africa is rich in the world of "might-have-beens." Historians have continued to ask the question of whether the strategy actually followed was the one most likely to win the war as quickly as possible; in this regard, an important new historical source was the revelation of the *Ultra* secret in the 1970s---referring to the ability to read the German *Enigma* code--- and its impact on the conduct of military operations in all theaters of war, including the Mediterranean and North Africa.

Carefully tended and peaceful cemeteries in Tobruk, El Alamein, Carthage, and Tunis are the saddest reminders of the combat that took place in the Libyan and Egyptian deserts, and the hills of Tunisia between 1940 and 1943. From North Africa, the war against Nazism and Fascism would move on to the continent of Europe.

2

Sources for Research on the War in North Africa, 1940-1943

PRINCIPAL RESEARCH COLLECTIONS

Public Record Office,
Ruskin Avenue,
Kew,
Richmond, Surrey, TW9 4DU
England

War Cabinet records are found in the CAB files; Prime Minister Winston Churchill's orders can be found in the PREM series. United War Diaries for Middle East forces are found under WO 169; Dominion Forces, WO 179; Field Marshal Earl Alexander of Tunis papers in WO 214. The Admiralty records (ADM series) contains valuable records on all aspects of the British naval effort in the Mediterranean. Operational records for the British Royal Air Force in North Africa are located in AIR 41.

Liddell Hart Centre for Military Archives,
King's College London,
Strand,
London WC2R 2LS
England

Includes B. H. Liddell Hart's own vast correspondence with many of the commanders involved in the North African campaign; Field Marshal Lord Alanbrooke papers (Chief of the Imperial General Staff); the General Sir Hastings Ismay papers (Churchill's military advisor); General Francis de Guingand papers (Montgomery's Chief of Staff); General Sir Richard O'Conner papers. Many other memoirs and papers relating to the war in the North Africa can also be found in the Liddell Hart Centre.

The Imperial War Museum
Lambeth Road
London SE1 6HZ
England

Contains the papers and war diary of Field Marshal Bernard L. Montgomery who assumed command of the British 8th Army in August 1942. With typical immodesty Monty noted in his diary, "If changes in the high command had not been made early in August, we would have lost Egypt . . . Actually, they were made just in time." The correspondence, as well as oral history interviews, of many other soldiers who fought in North Africa are deposited in the IWM and its Department of Sound Records. The researcher will find find a visit to the Museum's world famous photographic collection profitable.

Churchill Archives Centre
Churchill College
Cambridge CB3 0DS
England

Churchill papers; Stephen Roskill papers (Roskill was the author of the official British naval history of the war); Admiral Sir Bertram Ramsay papers; Vice-Admiral Sir James Somerville papers; correspondence for the biography of Admiral Sir Andrew Cunningham by author Oliver Warner; P. J. Grigg papers (his correspondence with Montgomery), and the papers of historian Ronald Lewin (biographer of Wavell, Rommel, and Montgomery); papers of Generals Alexander Galloway and T. W. Corbett, both of whom served under Auchinleck.

John Rylands Library
University of Manchester
150 Deansgate
Manchester M3 3EH
England

The papers of Field Marshal Claude Auchinleck; General Dorman O'Gowan (formerly Dorman-Smith) papers. Considering himself maligned in Winston Churchill's *The Hinge of Fate*, Dorman-Smith instituted libel action against Churchill.

Australian War Memorial
GPO Box 345
Canberra, ACT 2601
Australia

Unit war diaries; General Leslie Morshead papers (commander, 9th Australian Division); Field Marshal Sir Thomas Blamey papers; documents used by historians in writing the official Australian histories of their participation in the North African campaign.

Archivio Centrale dello Stato
Piazzale degli Archivi
Rome
Italy

    Correspondence of Marshal Graziani

Bundesarchiv/Militararchiv (central archives for military records/files)
Wiesentalstrasse 10
D-79115 Freiburg i. Br.
Federal Republic of Germany

Militargeschichtliches Forschungsamt (Military History Research Office)
Zepplinstrasse 127/128
D-14471 Potsdam
Federal Repubic of Germany

Bundesarchiv Koblenz
Potsdamerstrasse 1
D-56075 Koblenz
Federal Republic of Germany

    Contains files pertaining to OKH (Army High Command) and General Staff, personal papers of various generals, and documentary films/weekly newsreels.

Militarbibliothek Dresden
Olbrichtplatz 3
Postfach 100320
01073 Dresden
Federal Republic of Germany

United States Army Military History Institute
Carlisle Barracks
Pennsylvania 17013-5008

    Outstanding collection of papers of North African commanders: General Terry de la Mesa Allen papers (commander, 1st Infantry division); General Orlando Ward papers (commander, 1st Armored division); Colonel John K. Waters papers (1st

Armored regiment, 1st Armored division); Colonel Oscar Koch papers (Patton's chief Intelligence Officer); Interviews conducted by George F. Howe in writing the official US Army history, *The Mediterranean Theater of Operations, Northwest Africa: Seizing the Initiative in the West* [226], including frank comments by General George C. Marshall and Field Marshal Alexander of Tunis on individuals involved in the North African campaign; the Institute's oral history collection of World War II veterans contains responses pertinent to the campaign.

Manuscript Division
Library of Congress
Washington, D.C.

   The General George S. Patton, Jr., papers and General Carl Spaatz papers are useful for the Tunisian campaign.

Dwight D. Eisenhower Library, Abilene, Kansas

   General Dwight David Eisenhower was appointed Allied Supreme Commander of the *Torch* operation in August 1942. His correspondence includes that with generals Terry de la Mesa Allen, Charles W. Ryder, Montgomery, de Guingand, and other figures involved in North Africa; the Harry C. Butcher diary (Eisenhower's naval aide).

The Citadel Archives,
The Citadel,
The Military College of South Carolina,
Charleston, S.C. 29409

   The Mark Clark diary and other materials relating to his service in North Africa. The Museum contains informative and enjoyable exhibits, several relating to General Clark.

BIBLIOGRAPHIES AND GUIDES

Gwyn M. Bayliss, *Bibliographic Guide to the Two World Wars: An Annotated Survey of English-Language Reference Materials.* New York, 1978. [26].

Charles E. Dornbusch, *Unit Histories, Personal Narratives, United States Army: A Checklist.* [136].

A.G.S. Enser, *A Subject Bibliography of the Second World War: Books in English, 1939-1974.* Boulder, CO., [147].

A.G.S. Enser, *A Subject Bibliography of the Second World War: Books in*

English, 1975-1983. Boulder, CO., [148].

Allan M. Findlay, Anne M. Findlay, and Richard I. Lawless, *Tunisia*. Santa Barbara, CA., [157]. World Bibliographic Series, Clio Press.

Janet Foster and Julia Sheppard, *British Archives: A Guide to Archive Resources in the United Kingdom*. New York, 1989. [164].

Arthur L. Funk, *The Second World War: A Select Bibliography of Books in English since 1975*. Claremont, CA., 1985. [169].

Arthur L. Funk, *The Second World War: A Select Bibliography of Books in English 1980-1984*. Gainesville, FL., 1984. [170].

Robin Higham and Donald J. Mrozek, *A Guide to the Sources in U.S. Military History: Supplement III*. Hamden, Ct., 1993. [209].

Gerald Jordan, *British Military History: A Supplement to Robin Higham's Guide to the Sources*. New York, 1988. [248].

Ragai N. Makar, *Egypt*. Santa Barbara, CA., 1988. [314].

George S. Pappas, *United States Army Unit Histories*. Carlisle Barracks, PA., 1971. [366].

Eugene L. Rasor, *British Naval History since 1815: A Guide to the Literature*. New York, 1990. [391].

S. L. Mayer and W. J. Koenig, *The Two World Wars: A Guide to Manuscript Collections in the United Kingdom*. London, 1976. [324].

Myron J. Smith, Jr. *World War II: The European and Mediterranean Theaters: An Annotated Bibliography*. New York, 1984. [433].

Myron J. Smith, Jr. *World War II at Sea: A Bibiography of Sources in English:Vol. I: The European Theater*. 1976. [432].

Myron J. Smith, Jr. *Air War Bibliography, 1939-1945: English Language Sources. Vol. I: The European Theater*. [431].

Janet Ziegler, *World War II: Books in English, 1945-1965*. Stanford. CA., 1971. [503].

ATLASES

Vincent J. Esposito. *The West Point Atlas of American Wars. Vol. II, 1900-1953.* New York, 1959. [150].

Thomas E. Greiss, *Campaign Atlas to the Second World War.* Wayne,NJ., 1989. [191].

John Keegan. *The Times Atlas to the Second World War.* New York, 1989. [256].

Barrie Pitt and Frances Pitt, *The Month-By-Month Atlas of World War II.* New York, 1989 [377].

Peter Young, *Atlas of the Second World War.* New York, 1974. [501].

BIOGRAPHICAL DICTIONARIES

Philip V. Cannistraro, ed., *Historical Dictionary of Fascist Italy.* [71].

John Keegan, *Who Was Who in World War II.* [257].

David Mason, *Who's Who in World War II.* [318].

Chrisopher Tunney, *A Biographical Dictionary of World War II.* [470].

Elizabeth-Anne Wheal, Stephen Pope, and James Taylor, *A Dictionary of the Second World War.* [491].

ENCYCLOPEDIAS

Christopher Chant, *The Encyclopedia of Code Names of World War II.* [88].

R. Ernest Dupuy and Trevor N. Dupuy, *The Encyclopedia of Military History: From 3500 B.C. to the Present.* [140].

John Keegan, *Encyclopedia of World War II.* [255].

3

The Desert War, 1940-1942

STRATEGIC DECISIONS

World War II came to North Africa on June 10, 1940, when Benito Mussolini announced the coming declaration of war from the balcony of the Palazzo Venezia in Rome. In Libya, Italy's North African colony since 1912, fourteen Italian divisions numbering some 200,000 troops, under the command of Marshal Rudolfo Graziani, and at the end of a short sea rote from Sicily, prepared to strike a knock-out blow against the British Empire in the Middle East. Defending the British position in Egypt was General Archibald Wavell with a small force comprised of two divisions. Until the French armistice with Adolf Hitler in June, Italy's Libyan army had been held in check by the French Army of Africa in Tunisia; the combination of the French fleet with the British Mediterranean fleet had also matched Italy's considerable naval strength. After June, however, Italy's six battleships became the largest capital force in the Mediterranean. The Mediterranean was then closed to British merchant ships, and with Malta exposed to Italian air-attack, the British Mediterranean fleet withdrew to Alexandria.

A starting point for almost any study of World War II are the memoirs of Winston Churchill, although they must be used carefully since they do present, and very powerfully at that, his side of the question. The North African/ Mediterranean crisis of 1940 is discussed in *Their Finest Hour* [90], volume two in his *History of the Second World War*. Faced with the imminent invasion of Britain itself, Prime Minister Churchill made the first of his many momentous wartime decisions: Should Britain abandon the Mediterranean and Egypt? Churchill vetoed the proposal to withdraw the British Fleet from the Mediterranean---the Middle East would be held at all costs. At the height of the Battle of Britain, Churchill bravely dispatched half of Britain's few remaining tanks round the tip of Africa to reinforce the small British force in Egypt. Remarked Churchill, "The decision to give this blood transfusion while we braced ourselves to meet mortal danger was at once awful and right. No one faltered."

Neither was the aggressive British Commander in Chief of the Mediterranean Fleet ready to abandon that theater of war to the Axis powers. One of the great personal narratives of World War II, Admiral Andrew B. Cunningham's, *A Sailor's Odyssey*

[121], published in 1951, is a graphic and authoritative discussion of the Mediterranean conflict with vivid descriptions of the war at sea. Candid, unassuming and exciting, the memoir reflects the man. The Nelsonian Admiral is the subject of biographies by S.W.C. Pack, *Cunningham the Commander* [363], and Oliver Warner, *Cunningham of Hyndhope: Admiral of the Fleet* [483].

Neither at the time nor later was the decision to hold the Mediterranean without critics who doubted its wisdom: A.J.P. Taylor, the most controversial English historian of his age and author of the volume, *English History 1914-1945* [455], regarded the Mediterranean and North African war as a strategic blunder of the first magnitude. In Taylor's opinion, the Allies should never have fought there at all.

Churchill's decision to contest the Mediterranean is faulted by Correlli Barnett in his 1991 naval history *Engage the Enemy More Closely: The Royal Navy in the Second World War* [21]. As reviewer Dennis Showalter noted, Barnett is a superb narrator as well as a perceptive analyst. Never in its long history had the Royal Navy performed as gallantly and effectively as it did in World War II. The author argues, however, that the Mediterranean and North African campaign were not in Britain's best strategic interests.

O'CONNOR AND WAVELL

The Italian-British war began in earnest in September 1940 when Mussolini ordered an offensive into Egypt. After penetrating 60 miles into Egypt, Marshal Graziani halted, and stayed where he was for the next three months. In December, General Richard O'Connor, commanding one corps of British and Indian troops attacked the Italy army from the rear and in three days won a staggering victory, smashing three enemy corps at Sidi Barrani.

By February 1941, O'Connor's Western Desert Force had marched 500 miles to Beda Fomm in Libya, destroying ten enemy divisions and capturing 130,000 prisoners. A brief account, *Beda Fomm* [307] was written by military historian Kenneth Macksey for the Ballantine Illustrated History of World War II series.

The desert victories of O'Connor and General Archibald Wavell (Commander in Chief, Middle East) provided the British Empire with its first glimmer of sunlight during the darkest days of the war. Scholarship and literary style are combined in Barrie Pitt's book, *The Crucible of War: Western Desert 1941* [379], in which he synthesized archival sources, secondary works, and personal interviews to produce a spirited account of the first phase of the swirling, wide-open war in the Libyan desert. Pitt's perspective is British, but he includes a discussion of the Italian army and the Afrika Korps.

Other worthwhile studies are Cyril N. Barclay, *Against Great Odds: The Story of the First Offensive in Libya in 1940-41* [18], and the excellent Australian account by Gavin Long, *To Benghazi* [293].

The important part played by the British Royal Air Force is described by Arthur Longmore in his memoir, *From Sea to Sky, 1910-1945* [295]. The Australian-born Longmore commanded the British Middle Eastern Air Force in 1940-41. Denis

Richards and H. Saunders wrote the official British history, *The Royal Air Force 1939-1945* [396]. In the opening stage of the War in North Africa, the RAF was largely equipped with obsolete aircraft.

The first full-length biography of the friendly, small, and well-liked O'Connor, who in large part was responsible for the first significant British victory on land in World War II, appeared in 1989, under the apt title, *The Forgotten Victor: General Sir Richard O'Connor* [27], by Lt.-Col. Sir John Baynes. A helpful and brief synopsis of the campaign can be found in Barrie Pitt's essay on O'Connor in John Keegan, ed., *Churchill's Generals* [254].

What was called "Wavell's offensive" in 1940-41 set the pattern for fighting in the desert for the next two years---the rapid retreat along the single coast road by the defeated party, hotly pursued by the victor who attempted "hooks" inland through the desert to get behind the retreating enemy---which O'Connor's Western Desert Force had successfully accomplished at Beda Fomm on February 7, 1941, when the British 7th Armored Division had got ahead of and behind the retreating Italian army.

Archibald Wavell, once, briefly, a household name in Britain when his "Western Desert Force" destroyed Italian armies, has been the subject of several biographies. A two volume, intensely sympathetic biography was written by John Connell. The first volume, *Wavell: Scholar and Soldier* [108], covered his years in the Middle East. A former junior staff officer under Wavell, Connell's biography is an admiring, uncritical view of that fascinating and impressive one-eyed commander who edited an anthology of poetry during the war.

A more balanced assessment was offered by the military historian Ronald Lewin in his study, *The Chief: Field Marshal Lord Wavell, Commander-in-Chief and Viceroy, 1939-1947* [287]. Wavell's tragedy was that he was expected to defend the British Empire at the beginning of a war for which it was militarily unprepared. A man with great strength of character, Wavell did have his weaknesses, especially his desire to try and run a battle at very considerable distances when he knew neither the ground nor his subordinates.

The best and most recent biography of Wavell is that by Harold E. Raugh, Jr., *Wavell in the Middle East, 1939-1941: A Study in Generalship* [392]. Raugh brought to his biography a valuable measure of detachment, as well as an exhaustive bibliography, in his authoritative account of the laconic Wavell. In his foreword, Field Marshal Lord Carver, himself an outstanding military historian, comments that as a young officer serving in Wavell's command, "I, like most of my contemporaries, worshipped him as a hero." Wavell, like Carver himself, was a cultural product of the classical education of Winchester College.

A sympathetic essay on Wavell by Bernard Fergusson is to be found in *The War Lords* [76] edited by Michael Carver. Wavell's aide who served with him during the war was Peter Coats who authored, *Of Generals and Gardens: The Autobiography of Peter Coats* [100]. Coats, sophisticated and cosmopolitan, was the opposite of Wavell, an austere Wykehamist who could write well but suffered from a total lack of talk, small or serious. Wavell was noted for his "famous and formidable silences" which baffled even his admirers.

GREECE

Wavell and O'Connor's stunning victory against the Italians was short-lived, however. Eager to advance on Tripoli, O'Connor was ordered to stop; it was decided to send British help to Greece in the event of a German attack, and British assistance could only come from North Africa. Both at the time and in post-war years, O'Connor was convinced that he could have thrown the enemy out of his last foothold in North Africa, and thereby precluded a German foothold. Military historian B.H. Liddell Hart in his *History of the Second World War* [288] referred to the "golden opportunity of February 1941" that was reputedly missed when O'Connor was robbed of the necessary strength to sustain his advance on Tripoli. However, in his landmark work, *Ultra and Mediterranean Strategy* [32], Ralph Bennett offers a corrective to the optimism of O'Connor and others by pointing out that well before the Italians were bundled out of eastern Libya (Cyrenaica), Hitler had decided Italy could not be allowed to lose all its African territories, and to send a blocking force strong enough to stop the British and even launch local counterattacks, but no more.

Enormous controversy has surrounded the British decision to send what few veterans divisions there were in North Africa to assist Greece. Winston Churchill, a favorite target of critics, has received the lion's share of the blame. Historian John Charmley, in his provocative 1993 study, *Churchill: The End of Glory, A Political Biography* [89], echoes the charge of previous Churchill critics when he writes that British intervention in Greece "bore all the marks of a Churchill special."

In his study, *Anthony Eden: A Biography* [73], author David Carlton discusses the issue of British assistance to Greece. Eden was Churchill's Foreign Secretary. Carlton notes that by March 1941 Eden was enthusiastically for intervention whereas Churchill was "not sanguine about military success." The political biography, which Carlton honestly described as an "interim" work, is an essential supplement to Eden's own memoirs *The Reckoning*, published in 1965.

To date, the most complete scholarly treatment of Churchill's actions during the Greek episode is Sheila Lawlor's, *Churchill and the Politics of War 1940-41* [280]. The author argues that Churchill was willing to back away from intervention in Greece since he did not relish "another Norwegian fiasco." While acknowledging that Churchill was strong for intervention at the outset, the author argues that he became a "reluctant interventionist," who with characteristic resolution made the best of it after Foreign Secretary Anthony Eden signed an agreement with the Greek government, thus presenting Churchill and the Cabinet with a fait accompli. In any event, British and Dominion troops landed in Greece in March; faced with another unstoppable German blitzkrieg, they had to evacuate from Greece by the end of April.

The Greek decision is discussed thoroughly by Harold E. Raugh, Jr., in his book, *Wavell in the Middle East, 1939-1941: A Study in Generalship* [392], and by General Sir James Kennedy in his memoir, *The Business of War* [258].

HITLER COMES TO THE RESCUE

While British, New Zealand, and Australian divisions were leaving for Greece, Rommel and the Afrika Korps arrived in North Africa. Hitler selected Rommel and a small German force of two divisions for Operation *Sonnenblume* (Sunflower), the effort to rescue the Italians in Libya. Initially the Germans saw their intervention as strictly defensive, against what seemed as if it might be an imminent British attack on Tripoli.

On February 12, 1941 Rommel flew to Tripoli, setting foot on African soil for the first time. He did not know of the British decision to withdraw forces from North Africa in order to send them to Greece. Launching a surprise attack (to his own side as well as the British) with a handful of troops and dummy tanks---dummies mounted on Volkswagens---Rommel began a campaign that by the end of April had swept the British out of Libya, except for a small force shut up in Tobruk.

TOBRUK

Between 1941 and 1942, the small Libyan port of Tobruk became something of a symbol of victory or defeat for the forces fighting in North Africa. In the space of seven months, in 1941-42, Tobruk witnessed two great battles, a British victory and a British defeat. Soldier and accomplished military historian Michael Carver fought in both battles. When published in 1964, Carver's study, *Tobruk* [81], was called the "definitive" study on the subject. A General in the British army at the time of *Tobruk's* publication, the author would go on to become a Field Marshal.

In his account, Carver considered the reasons for the difference between the first battle and the second when the British were comparatively stronger. He believed that British tank commanders, under the combined influence of T.E. Lawrence (Lawrence of Arabia) and B.H. Liddell Hart, carried dispersion of armor to excess. He thought the Germans' great advantages were in their better combined arms tactics and, in the second battle, better generalship. Carver was critical of Rommel's conduct of the *Crusader* battle; the best example of where he snatched defeat from the jaws of victory. His conduct of the second battle, at Gazala, showed a great improvement.

Carver asked the sensitive but necessary question, why did the 9th Australian Division, and later the 70th British Division, hold Tobruk for eight months and the 2nd South African Division lose it in two days? The author's answer was that Rommel attacked the wrong way in the first case and the right way in the second. He attacked Tobruk's point of strongest defense in 1941; the second time, in June 1942, he attacked where the anti-tank ditch was at its shallowest. The attacks came against two experienced formations, the 11th Indian Brigade and the 201st Guards Brigade. Carver's superbly written account contained vivid quotations from unit histories and autobiographies.

During Tobruk's eight month siege, the defenders were Australian, British, Czech, Indian, and Polish. When a newspaper headline declared, "Tobruk can take it!" General Leslie Morshead of the 9th Australian Division reacted angrily, "We're not here to take it, --- We're here to give it!" Morshead made it quite clear to his men that there would be no withdrawal from Tobruk. The Australian general is the subject of a biography by J.H. Moore, *Morshead—A Biography of Lieutenant-General Sir Leslie Morshead* [338].

Many accounts have been written describing the siege of Tobruk; among the essential sources are Barton Maughan, *Tobruk and El Alamein* (official Australian history) [321]; W.E. Murphy, *Relief of Tobruk* (official New Zealand history) [348]; Chester Wilmot, *Tobruk* [494]; Timothy Hall, *Tobruk 1941: The Desert Siege* [195]; Anthony Heckstall-Smith, *Tobruk: The Story of a Siege* [205]; James W. Stock, *Tobruk: The Siege* [447]; A. C. Willison, *The Relief of Tobruk* [493]; Jan Yindrich, *Fortress Tobruk* [499]; David Jablonski, *The Desert Warriors: The Battle for North Africa 1940-1943* [235]; Gordon Lansborough, *Tobruk Commando* [277]; Jack Coggins, *Campaign for North Africa* [103]; and Barrie Pitt's four-part "Tobruk" series in *British Heritage* [381], a concise treatment with well choosen photographs.

German accounts include *The Rommel Papers* [290] edited by B.H. Liddell Hart; F.W. von Mellenthin, *Panzer Battles* [478]; H.W. Schmidt, *With Rommel in the Desert* [416]; Albert Kesselring, *The Memoirs of Field-Marshal Kesselring* [260]; Paul Carrell, *The Foxes of the Desert* [72]; and Adalbert von Taysen's, *Tobruk 1941: Der Kampf in Nordafrika* [479], volume 21 of the excellent series, Germany in World War II, published by the German Military History Research Office.

DESERT BATTLES: *BATTLEAXE, CRUSADER,* AND *GAZALA*

Rommel's advance had dangerously stretched his line of supply from Tripoli, and Wavell launched a counter-offensive in mid-June 1941 codenamed *Battleaxe*, a costly defeat. An outstanding critical study of military operations in North Africa from the *Crusader* battle of 1941 to the capture of Tunis, is that by General Sir Francis Tuker. His book, *Approach to Battle* [469], which was published in 1962, was "a serious attempt to let others know why it was that Eighth Army lost its battles and why it was that it won them." Military historian Ronald Lewin, called Tuker, who commanded the outstanding 4th Indian Division, "perhaps the most intelligent and percipient" of the British divisional commanders in World War II. An iconoclast, critical of all sacred taboos, Tuker provided a penetrating analysis of British shortcomings, in the area of training, equipment, and high command. In his opinion, the British possessed third-rate tanks and ineffective, two-pounder anti-tank "pop-guns." While a number of Tuker's judgments may be questioned, *Approach to Battle* is a very good book indeed.

An excellent survey of the North African campaign is the 1975 account, *The Battle for North Africa 1940-43* [237] by General W.G.F. Jackson who served in the theater as a young officer. He analyses the three phases of the war: Wavell's period, Rommel's exploits, and the Tunisian campaign. He comments that in the last phase the Allied force floundered on the edge of disaster when faced with German professionalism. He does not indict the troops for British defeats in the desert, but he argues that almost without exception British generalship was amateur and often incompetent. A stimulating evaluation of the war, Jackson's central point is that democracies need time to find "their own type of Rommel."

British artillery is the subject of Brigadier Shelford Bidwell's, *Gunners at War: A Tactical Study of the Royal Artillery in the Twentieth Century* [40]. Highly critical of what he regarded as the misuse of artillery in the early stages of the Desert War, Bidwell claims that the lessons of World War I had to be learned all over again in the Second, particularly the necessity to concentrate artillery. The author contended that a frontal attack could succeed if artillery fire is concentrated instead of dispersed.

The British defeat in *Battleaxe* undermined Wavell's position, and he was replaced by the Indian army's leading soldier, General Claude Auchinleck, on July 5, 1941. Auchinleck's aim was to relieve Tobruk and recapture Cyrenaica, as a first step to driving the Axis out of Libya. Operation *Crusader*, as his winter offensive was codenamed, began on November 18 with nearly 700 tanks against 400 Axis. A first attempt to raise the siege of Tobruk failed, and with British armored forces scattered around the desert Rommel believed the British to be within inches of defeat.

David Fraser describes Rommel's actions in *Knight's Cross: A Life of Field Marshal Erwin Rommel* [166]. Nobody was superior to Rommel in exploiting an enemy's confusion; by moving eastward with his surving tanks, he believed he could swing around the southern flank of the invading British forces and eventually destroy them. On November 24, Rommel set off eastward at the head of the 21st Panzer Division, followed by the 15th Panzer Division, in what came to be known as "the dash to the wire---a thrust to be made without troubling about what happened to his flanks. The "dash to the wire" was intended to cut off the entire British Imperial Army from Egypt.

War correspondent Alan Moorehead described the confused state of the 8th Army in his classic work, *African Trilogy* [339]. In the book's introduction, Lord Wavell said that it was in many respects "the truest tale of all." Moorehead closely and accurately observed the desert war with all those human ingredients so often left out of academic history.

General Sir Alan Cunningham, commanding the British 8th Army, believed that his army faced disaster from Rommel's thrust and he urged withdrawal back to Libya. Auchinleck, exhibiting what Moorehead called "a touch of brilliance and moral courage" at this grim moment, flew to the battlefront and despite British heavy tank losses he refused to order retreat. *Crusader* would go on. The game was over for Rommel who had scented confusion among the British and sought to exploit the situation; but this was not Caporetto in 1917 when his daring had led to success against the Italians. Realizing how dangerous his position was, Rommel withdrew westward. By December the British relieved Tobruk, its garrison now made up of British and Polish troops which had replaced the 9th Australian Division.

The British had won *Crusader* on points, not the expected knockout; British preponderance in material permitted them to win the battle of attrition after three weeks of wildly confused combat and maneuvering. Robert Crisp, a tank commander in the battles around Sidi Rezegh describes the hot and fast action in his memoir,

Brazen Chariots: An Account of Tank Warfare in the Western Desert, November-December 1941 [118]. In the fighting, Rommel's concentrated armor had destroyed in piecemeal fashion the widely scattered British armored units. The 7th Armored Division had crossed into Libya with 450 tanks; only days later the number was reduced to less than 130.

Following the *Crusader* battle, Rommel retreated to El Agheila, some 500 miles to the west, from where he had begun his offensive the previous March.

Rommel's side of the story is found in *The Rommel Papers* [290]. The battle is described in *Crusader: The Eighth Army's Forgotten Victory, November 1941-January 1942* [228] by Richard Humble. The famous "Desert Rats" of the 7th Armored Division were in the thick of the fight: George Forty, in his lavishly illustrated volume, *Desert Rats at War* [161], called Sidi Rezegh the 7th Armored Divisions's "finest hour." Through pictures, Forty captures what life was like for British soldiers in the desert war. G.L. Verney's, *The Desert Rats: The Story of the 7th Armoured Division* [476], traces the Division's wartime operations. Robin Neillands, *The Desert Rats: 7th Armoured Division, 1940-1945* [351], was published in 1991.

Rommel struck again on January 21, 1942, gaining a bigger surprise than the previous spring. With the British 8th Army supply line overextended (500 miles west of Tobruk), and weakened by the loss of two battle-hardened Australian divisions transferred to the Far East and replaced by two less veteran divisions, Rommel forced the British back to Gazala.

During the spring, both sides in the desert made good their losses; while Auchinleck prepared to go on the offense, Rommel anticipated him and attacked on May 27, 1942. The Battle of Gazala which followed marked the highpoint of German military professionalism and the nadir of British military competence during the desert war. Not even the courage and endurance of the soldiers could make up for the tactical and command weaknesses of the British.

At Bir Hacheim (a "Dorn im Fleische" to Rommel until its final capture), General Pierre Koenig and his Free French Brigade made an epic stand at the most exposed and isolated sector of the British front. Koenig describes the battle in his 1951 account, *Bir Hacheim* [273]. An excellent Ballantine paperback by Richard Holmes, *Bir Hacheim: Desert Citadel* [217], connects the battle with the political scene. He claims that while Bir Hacheim was a military defeat, in a political sense it was a victory since it gave the Free French movement led by Charles de Gaulle credibility.

In an area known as the Cauldron, British tanks charged to their death against the enemy's anti-tank guns. John Agar-Hamilton and L.C.F. Turner in the excellent South African official history, *Crisis in the Desert, May to July 1942* [2] provide a very illuminating account of the "Cauldron battle." A regimental and divisional approach is taken by South African Neil Orpen in his account *War in the Desert* [360]. The author is not afraid to criticize and there are many illustrations and photographs of South African soldiers at work or in action.

Antony Brett-James, *Ball of Fire: The Fifth Indian Division in the Second World War* [57], is highly critical of the tactics used in the Gazala battle. He commanded an

Indian brigade in the fighting.

The British defeat at Gazala culminated in the capture of Tobruk on June 21. Lost was the entire 2nd South African Division, together with one British and one Indian brigade. After the brilliant and protracted defense of Tobruk in 1941, its surrender in 1942 after only one week of siege, came as a bitter blow to the Allied cause and greatly strengthened Axis morale. After Gazala, Rommel wrote to his wife, "a wonderful battle."

Flying up to the front, Auchinleck took personal command of the 8th Army from General Neil Ritchie (he had unwisely appointed Ritchie after Cunningham's removal), an action which probably saved that Army and Egypt for the British. The comments of Prime Minister Churchill can be found in *The Hinge of Fate* [92]: "He should have done this when I asked him to in May."

ULTRA AND INTELLIGENCE

The very existence of Ultra---the intelligence derived from decoding Axis Enigma messages--- remained a closely guarded secret until the 1970s. The first volume of the British Official History, by F. H. Hinsley (and others), *British Intelligence in the Second World War* [215], contains authoritative information on the breaking of the German Enigma code and on the early use of *Ultra*. Beginning with a group of under 100, by 1944 over 7,000 people were involved in *Ultra* decoding work at Bletchley Park outside London.

In 1989 appeared the landmark study, *Ultra and Mediterranean Strategy* [32], by Ralph Bennett. The author had been one of the young "professor-type" scholars who staffed Hut 3 at Bletchley Park where all German army and air signals were translated and decoded. At the time Bennett was recruited as a codebreaker, he was a young Cambridge professor with a year's study of medieval history at Munich University.

In his insightful review article "Ralph Bennett and the Study of Ultra," *Intelligence and National Security* [155], historian John Ferris declared that Bennett's book has "immediately become the standard work on *Ultra* in the Mediterranean theater of operations between 1941-45, superseding even *British Intelligence* (by Hinsley)."

In North Africa and the Mediterranean, writes Bennett, *Ultra* "won its spurs, so to speak." Until the summer of 1942, *Ultra's* most valuable contribution was the information that it provided on Axis convoys to North Africa. If Rommel had obtained those supplies that were sunk because of the information provided by *Ultra*, Bennett thinks he would have won the *Crusader* battle, captured Tobruk, and driven the 8th Army back to the Nile. The author states that not until the summer of 1942, did *Ultra* provide consistently reliable intelligence to the desert Army commanders, first Auchinleck, then Montgomery.

On the German side, Bennett observes that Rommel benefitted greatly from two intelligence sources. First, information from the intercepted reports of the American military attaché in Cairo, Colonel Bonner Fellers. The British gave Fellers detailed information about upcoming offensives, which was heavily supported by American material. Second, Rommel received information from Captain Alfred Seebohm's

Third Radio Intercept Company, which provided up-to-the-minute tactical information based on intercepts of British army signals. Every evening Rommel looked at the intercept reports of Captain Seebohm's interception unit.

Bennett makes the strong case that between them, these two sources inspired many of his best thrusts between January and June 1942, but both dried up when his exhausted army reached the El Alamein defenses. Suspecting that their code was compromised, the Americans changed it at the end of June; Captain Seebohm's interception unit was destroyed and its files captured by the 9th Australian Division at Tell el Eisa early in July.

Reminiscences of some two dozen of the Ultra codebreakers can be found in F.H. Hinsley and Alan Stripp, editors, *Codebreakers: The Inside Story of Bletchley Park* [214].

In the vast distances of North Africa, the only means of communication was by wireless/radio communication. The British army's communications in North Africa is the subject of an important 1990 article by John Ferris, "The British Army, Signals and Security in the Desert Campaign, 1940-42." *Intelligence and National Security* [156]. He shows how the "flimsy security" of British communications provided Rommel (through Seebohm's interceptions) with information equivalent in value to that of *Ultra*. Ferris comments ruefully that the bill for inter-war neglect fell due in 1940. Shortage of radio equipment, few trained personnel, and over-confidence in signals security after defeating the Italians, were just some of the weaknesses that were "tailor-made" to suit Rommel. In one aspect of signal warfare the British were fortunate; a number of Palestinian Jews, refugees from Nazi Germany and knowledgeable about the German army and its slang, served as British army radio operators.

In contrast to the unprepard British, the German army possessed as the beginning of the war what Ferris calls "the finest signals service of any army on earth." Rommel, declares Ferris, did not need the genius of Napoleon to win in the desert in 1941 "He merely needed the British Army as his enemy." The *Battleaxe* defeat is attributed in large part to failures in British signals security. Too often, British commanders, losing faith in their men and themselves, desperately trying to regain control of a battle, "reached for the radio telephone like drowning men." The more intense and confused the battle, the more likely they were to speak in uncoded, plain language. If *Ultra* was the most sophisticated form of signals intelligence in World War II, the interception of plain language transmissions was the simplest. Ferris argues that Rommel gained as much from the latter as any Allied commander ever gained from former. British signals security did improve radically, but Ferris thinks the most important reason for the improvement was brought about when the British army ceased to make war as Rommel wished. By deliberately slowing down the pace of battle, Montgomery reduced the level of confusion on the battlefield, which led in turn to less desperate use of the radio by British commanders, hence to greater signals security.

A valuable contribution on the role of specialized forces in North Africa is the study by John W. Gordon, *The Other Desert War: British Special Forces in North Africa, 1940-1943* [185]. Gordon's book focuses on the Long Range Desert Group

(LRDG) although he also examines the activities of the Special Air Services (SAS). The author points out that direct "behind-the-lines" observation of the movement of Axis forces by the LRDG filled in gaps left by *Ultra*; just as important, LRDG watchers provided corroboration of *Ultra* information and confirmed that the enemy were not using their radio traffic to provide inaccurate information to unsuspecting *Ultra* eavesdroppers. Gordon's study is a welcome reminder of the importance of all sources of intelligence in war, not just signals intelligence.

Other important sources on the unconventional side of the desert war are W.B.K.Shaw's, *Long Range Desert Group: The Story of its Work in Libya 1940-1943* [423]; R.L. Kay's, *Long Range Desert Group in Libya, 1940-41* [251], part of the New Zealand Official History series; the autobiography *Private Army* [371] by Vladimir Peniakoff who founded his famous Private Army for long range penetration behind the enemy lines; Arthur Swinson's *The Raiders:Desert Strike Force* [454] was a Ballantine War Book. Len Deighton has a short essay, "The Private Armies," in *Alamein and the Desert War* [245]. If unconventional units were extremely useful at gathering Intelligence, they had less success in such raids as that on Rommel at Breda Littoria on the night of November 17-18, 1941. Although a very brave action, no one stopped to wonder if the hard-driving Rommel would be 200 miles behind the frontlines!

A very detailed and uncritical assessment of Rommel's intelligence sources is described in Hans-Otto Behrendt's book, *Rommel's Intelligence in the Desert Campaign, 1941-1943* [29].

AUCHINLECK

After a visit to Egypt, Churchill decided to make changes in the British high command, and on August 15 he replaced Auchinleck with General Sir Harold Alexander as commander-in-chief Middle East; General Bernard Montgomery was simultaneously appointed to command the 8th Army.

Concerned over a possible German threat to Persia and Iraq from the north, Auchinleck had been unwilling to accept Churchill's demand that he focus all of his efforts on defeating Rommel. In a letter that he wrote after his removal, Auchinleck continued to insist that the Persian Gulf far outweighed Egypt in strategic importance, and if one or the other had to be sacrificed, "the Persian Gulf is the one to hold."

Whatever the merits of Auchinleck's strategic and command decisions, there has been general consensus regarding his high-principled character. Churchill remarked that removing him was like "shooting a noble stag." In his 90s, Auchinleck lived in retirement in Morocco and died in Marrakech on March 23, 1981.

In his massive biography *Auchinleck* [107] published in 1959, John Connell was largely uncritical of Auchinleck. The author was emphatic that Auchinleck had decisively defeated Rommel in July 1942; consequently, July 1942, not October 1942 when Montgomery won his victory, was the "real turning point of World War II."

Despite having access to British official papers released since Connell's work, Roger Parkinson's 1977 biography, *The Auk: Auchinleck, Victor at Alamein* [368], is a highly partisan study and not an objective reassessment of the "Auk." In Parkinson's version, his hero who saved the day at "First Alamein" in July is unfairly dismissed and never given credit for his victory by an ungrateful Churchill. Michael Carver reviewed Parkinson's biography for the *Times Literary Supplement* [80]. Carver, a veteran of El Alamein, a Field Marshal, and the author of books of enduring value (*El Alamein* and *Tobruk*, which are both discussed elsewhere in this bibliography) on the War in North Africa, regretted the bitter partisanship that was all too often displayed by writers on the subject of the war in the desert. Much of the blame, wrote Carver, must be laid at the door of Montgomery himself who treated Auchinleck with scorn in contrast to the restrained and gentlemanly behavior of the latter.

Critical of the biography's subtitle, "Victor at Alamein," Carver felt there was danger that "the pendulum will swing too far the other way," from Auchinleck being given too little credit for the July actions to the other extreme of being given too much. Carver claimed that everybody in the desert at that time regarded Auchinleck's chief of staff T.W. Corbett as "hopelessly incompetent," and almost everyone distrusted the "unreliable and unrealistic"deputy chief of staff General Eric E. "Chink" Dorman-Smith.

Lavinia Greacen offers a defense of Dorman-Smith in her book, *Chink: A Biography* [187]. Some critics referred to Dorman-Smith as Auchinleck's "evil genius."

Philip Warner's 1981 biography *Auchinleck: The Lonely Soldier* [483] is a hagiographic account that praises the "Auk" extravagantly. Warner asserted that Auchinleck was the best British general in World War II. Other accounts favorable toward Auchinleck include Peter Bates, *Dance of War: The Story of the Battle of Egypt* [24], and Donald G Brownlow, *Checkmate at Ruweisat: Auchinleck's Finest Hour* [63].

In his 1985 memoir, *Flashback: A Soldier's Story* [398], General Charles Richardson strongly condemned the effort to glorify Auchinleck's July 1942 "piecemeal" attacks by calling them "The First Battle of Alamein." In 1942, Richardson was a young officer on the 8th Army planning staff. Richardson doubted that Auchinleck could have turned the tide, no matter what new resources might have come his way. "We youngsters," declared Richardson, "felt that the removal of Auchinleck was essential."

The views of Dominion commanders about the competence of British leadership in the summer of 1942 are mentioned in D.M. Horner's, *High Command: Australia and Allied Strategy 1939-1945* [218].

New Zealander H.K. Kippenberger wrote an extremely frank memoir about his Desert War experiences: in his book *Infantry Brigadier* [266], Kippenberger criticized orders which wasted the lives of troops in badly coordinated attacks. He declared that there was a "most intense distrust, almost hatred of our armor." When the question arose of pulling back to the Nile, Kippenberger protested that it would be "criminal to give up Egypt to 25,000 German troops and 100 tanks."

Official national histories and other sources on the crisis in the summer of 1942 include R.J. Taylor, *Kiwis in the Desert: The North African Campaign, 1940-1943* [458]; Compton Mackenzie, *Eastern Epic. Vol. I: September 1939-March 1943* [305]; Barton Maughan, *Tobruk and El Alamein: Australia in the War of 1939-1945* [321]; P.C. Bharucha, *The North African Campaign, 1940-1943* [38], describes the important Indian contribution. During World War II, the Indian Empire raised the greatest volunteer army in history. The official New Zealand history, *Battle for Egypt* [420], was written by J.L. Scoullar; John Agar-Hamilton and L.C.F. Turner, analyzed the summer disaster in the official South African history, *Crisis in the Desert: May to July 1942* [2]. In the official British history by I.S.O. Playfair, *British Fortunes reach their Lowest (September 1941 to September 1942)* [382], the author, who was not a fan of Montgomery's, referred to the July 1942 battles as "First Ruweisat" (July 14-17) and "Second Ruweisat" (July 21 and 22), not "First Alamein."

Playfair served as consultant to the volume produced by Horizon magazine, *Desert War in North Africa* [421] by Stephen W. Sears. Numerous photographs add to the book's interest.

CORRELLI BARNETT

In his bibliographical essay, "Fifty Books on the Second World War," which is found in his outstanding survey *The Second World War*, military historian John Keegan commented that much has been written on the war in the North Africa, but nowhere better than in Correlli Barnett's classic work, *The Desert Generals* [22]. Published in 1960, *The Desert Generals* set off a firestorm of controversy, largely because of its radical reappraisal of Field Marshal Bernard L. Montgomery by the youthful Barnett.

In the 1981 preface to the second edition, Barnett noted that *The Desert Generals* was written at a time "when the Montgomery myth held almost unchallenged sway" over public opinion. *The Desert Generals* had been a full-broadside reply to the Field Marshal's *Memoirs* [337] published in 1958. In his account, Barnett argued that Auchinleck's victory in July 1942 at "first Alamein" was "the true turning-point" in the North African campaign. He also strongly rejected Churchill's statement that "Before Alamein [Montgomery's victory] we never had a victory. After Alamein we never had a defeat."

In *The Desert Generals*, Barnett was not blind to Auchinleck's mistakes, acknowledging his poor judgment in appointing first Cunningham ---"He was rather like the successful owner of a village shop suddenly put in charge of a London department store"--- then Ritchie to command the 8th Army. Barnett's essay on Auchinleck in Michael Carver's 1976 study, *The War Lords: Military Commanders of the Twentieth Century* [76], is a perceptive assessment of the "Auk."

Five years after the publication of *The Desert Generals*, Barnett acknowledged to General Richard O'Connor, the hero of Sidi Barrrini and Beda Fomm, that "at this distance I would agree with you that I was too obviously critical of Monty." At the time *The Desert Generals* was written, however, he was writing "in the teeth of the all the wartime and postwar adulation and distortion, when Monty's reputation was absolutely unblemished."

Part defense of General Ritchie and part reassessment of the Libyan campaign, Michael Carver takes both the pro-Auchinleck and pro-Montgomery camps to task in his 1986 book, *Dilemmas of the Desert War: A New Look at the Libyan Campaign 1940-1942* [77]. While faulting Montgomery for being "grossly unfair" to Auchinleck who had held Rommel in July at the Alamein line, Carver is highly critical of Auchinleck's actions beforehand. Apart from the example Auchinleck set of resolution, determination, and calm, Carver sees little evidence of exceptional foresight, skill or judgment.

MALTA

With Italy's entry in the war, the island of Malta, located almost exactly in the center of the Mediterranean, took on enormous significance as the only British base in the 2,000 mile stretch of sea between Gibraltar and Alexandria. Only 20 minutes flying time (60 miles south) from Sicily, and under the British flag since in 1800, Malta served as a refuge and refueling point for British warships or merchant ships midway between Gibraltar and Alexandria, as well as a base from which to attack Italian convoys crossing the so-called "Sicilian Narrows," the less than 100 miles of water between Sicily and Tunisia.

An essential Italian source on the central role of Malta in the North African war is Mariano Gabriele's, *Operazione C 3: Malta* [174], a volume in the Italian official history series. In Italy's favor were the short sea routes to the Libyan ports of Tripoli, Benghazi, and Tobruk, and the closeness of Axis land-based aircraft to Malta, as well as that of the Italian battlefleet. The British fleet at Alexandria was at least two days' steaming time away from Malta.

Blocking the Axis sea routes to North Africa, a vulnerable Malta drew down on itself a crushing Axis air bombardment. The Axis siege of Malta was one of the longest and grimmest campaigns of World War II.

In his 1970 book, *Siege Within The Walls: Malta 1940-1943* [373], Steward Perowne credits Churchill with the decision to hold Malta: "But to one man the overall situation remained clear, the overriding necessity of maintaining Malta vital, and that man was Churchill."

Winner of the New Hampshire Book Prize for 1984, Charles A. Jellison in his study, *Besieged: The World War II Ordeal of Malta, 1940-1942* [244], argued, as other scholars have done, that "the island was the determining factor in the contest for control of the Mediterranean and North Africa." It provisioned British planes on their way to Egypt, occupied the attention of Axis aircraft that might otherwise have been used in North Africa, and provided the British with a base from which to destroy Axis shipping. Jellison's account is revisionist in its portrayal of a people forced into a conflict not directly theirs. He stresses the relative indifference of the British to the welfare of the Maltese they were supposed to be protecting. In his review of Jellison's book, military historian Dennis Showalter observed that the author tended to accept uncritically the perspective of Maltese nationalists.

A prolific British author of popular naval history, Ernle Bradford wrote the 1985 account, *Siege: Malta, 1940-1943* [53]. The author covers all the major military engagements as well as such topics as the incidence of pro-Fascist sentiment among the Maltese and the high rate of malnutrition during the worst of the siege. For general readers, the book is thoroughly researched and readable.

The British navy's role in sustaining Malta is told by Correlli Barnett in his stirring account, *Engage the Enemy More Closely: The Royal Navy in the Second World War* [21]. Barnett seeks to demonstrate that the British Empire, with its oceanic communications, was less a source of strength to Britain than of weakness. Never afraid of challenging sacred historical canons, Barnett refers to Malta as "that strategic burden and moral obligation glorified into a heroic myth." Because of the many British ships sunk or damaged during the struggle to sustain the island of Malta, he describes the costly naval effort in the central Mediterranean as "The Verdun of Maritime War."

The article, "The Resupply of Malta in World War II," *Naval War College Review*, by Dora Alves explains why the longtime base of the British Mediterranean fleet was not well prepared militarily to withstand the Axis onslaught. Little was done before the war to prepare Malta's defenses because its proximity to Italian airfields and naval bases was thought to make the island indefensible. The island's defenses in part consisted of three obsolete biplanes, nicknamed "Faith," "Hope," and "Charity."

The late naval historian Stephen Roskill wrote the monumental official British history *The War at Sea, 1939-1945* [407]. Volumes one and two in the series describe the Royal Navy's enormous effort in the Mediterranean. The ordeal and heroic contribution made by merchant seamen to Malta's survival is conveyed in Roskill's account, *A Merchant Fleet in War* [406]

Ian Cameron's *Red Duster, White Ensign: The Story of the Malta Convoys* [70] is the story of the convoys which had to fight their way through Axis air, submarine, and surface attacks. Only half of the sixty supply ships dispatched in 1942 arrived safely in Malta.

Gordon W. Stead's *A Leaf Upon the Sea: A Small Ship in the Mediterranean, 1941-1943* [440] is the fascinating story of Canadian in the Royal Navy who participated in the central Mediterranean naval campaign. The desperate situation on Malta led Churchill to ask Roosevelt if USS *Wasp* could carry British Spitfire fighter planes to the island. The events are described in Churchill's *The Hinge of Fate* [92]. The American carrier made two trips to Malta, leading a delighted Churchill to signal, "Who said a wasp couldn't sting twice?"

The famous Operation *Pedestal* convoy of August 11-13 1942 is described by Peter Shankland and Anthony Hunter in *Malta Convoy* [422]: under almost continuous Axis attack by submarines, torpedo boats, and aircraft, only five out of the fourteen merchant ships in the convoy reached Malta, while several warships were damaged or sunk. The arrival of the American owned oil tanker *Ohio*, though severely damaged and only kept afloat by the tremendous efforts of the ship's crew and helping escort vessels, was particularly important.

British submarine activities in the central Mediterranean campaign are described by a former submarine commander in *British Submarines at War 1939-1945* [316] by Alastair Mars.

British naval operations off the Libyan coast in 1941 are described by S.W.C. Pack in his book *The Battle of Sirte* [365]. The RAF commander on Malta was Air Marshal Sir Hugh Lloyd who wrote the account, *Briefed to Attack: Malta's Part in African Victory* [291]. British Air Marshal Arthur Tedder praised Lloyd for his part in the island's defense. In April 1942, the Axis air forces flew some 4,900 sorties against Malta; the air raid sirens sounded 275 times in Valetta, the island's capital---an average of once every 2 1/2 hours throughout that grim month. The air war is described by John Terraine in his book, *Right of the Line* [461].

The story of a Canadian fighter pilot on Malta is told by George F. Beurling and Leslie Roberts in *Malta Spitfire* [36]. Howard M. Coffin's, *Malta Story* [102] is the story of an American in the RAF who fought on Malta. The famous fighter planes that helped to save the island receive the attention of Christopher Shores, Brian Cull and Nicola Malizia in *Malta: The Hurricane Years, 1940-41* [424], and *Malta: The Spitfire Year 1942* [426].

Captain Lewis Ritchie's *Epic of Malta* [400] contains photographs and paintings of the bombed and battered island whose people were awarded the George Cross in April 1942 for their heroism. Joseph's *When Malta Stood Alone* [331] is largely based on Maltese newspaper records. An eyewitness description of the siege is *Malta-The Thorn in Rommel's Side: Six Months that Turned the War* [299] by Laddie Lucas.

THE LOGISTIC AND STRATEGIC DEBATE

Should Malta have been taken first in July 1942 before Rommel launched his drive on Cairo? The merits of this decision have been endlessly debated. An essential source is the memoir of Admiral Erich Raeder, *My Life* [388] who served as Hitler's naval Commander in Chief. He repeatedly urged Hitler to sieze the island, which Raeder called the "British wasp nest at Malta." In Raeder's opinion, the decision not to invade Malta in July 1942 was a fatal mistake.

The German Mediterranean theater commander was Field Marshal Albert Kesselring. He expressed his side of the story in *The Memoirs of Field-Marshal Kesselring* [260]. Kesselring believed that the Axis had to safeguard their supply lines to North Africa by "smoking out that hornet's nest." He too called the decision not to seize Malta, but instead to drive towards Cairo, a "fundamental blunder."

In his book *Hitler's Mistakes* [283], military historian Ronald Lewin called Hitler's failure to seize Malta "another major mistake," since the island's loss would have been a blow to the British on an "immeasurable scale." Axis possession of Malta would have prevented attacks on Rommel's lifeline.

A provocative reinterpretation of Malta's impact on Rommel's supply situation was presented by Israeli military historian Martin Van Creveld in his highly acclaimed 1977 study, *Supplying War: Logistics From Wallenstein to Patton* [475]. Rommel's

North African campaign was one of those operations selected by Van Creveld for assessing the effects of logistics upon strategy. According to Van Creveld, despite Rommel's tactical brilliance, he was "himself largely to blame" for the supply problems of the Afrika Korps by irresponsibly overextending his lines of communication. The author concluded that Malta did not really interfere that much with Rommel's seaborne supply line. He argued that the much-maligned Italians were able to ship practically everything the Afrika Korps needed, but that the troops failed to receive much of it; Van Creveld estimated that Axis vehicles used 30 to 50 per cent of the fuel landed just driving back and forth between Tripoli and the frontline, a round-trip of over 2,000 miles. North Africa suffered from even worse transport facilities than those found in Russia! Hitler's tolerance of Rommel's repeated attempts to advance beyond his supply lines was, in Van Creveld's opinion, "hopelessly wrong."

HERKULES

In January 1942, the Axis considered a Crete-style invasion of Malta, codenamed *Herkules* (Hercules). Rommel flew to see Hitler in February, urging on a reluctant Fuhrer the need to remove this thorn in his army's side. Hitler's views are described by General Walter Warlimont, Deputy Chief of the Wehrmacht operations staff, in his essay, "The Decision in the Mediterranean 1942." in *Decisive Battles of World War II: The German View* [240], edited by H.A. Jacobsen and J. Rohwer, as well as in his memoir, *Inside Hitler's Headquarters* [482]. In April, Hitler and Mussolini agreed to Rommel's plea to seize Malta, but in the aftermath of Tobruk, Rommel changed his mind and asked for permission to drive on Cairo first. Mussolini, however, wrote to Hitler on June 21st urging him to attack Malta before going further. In the enthusiasm of the moment, Hitler supported Rommel and insisted that "a historic turning point" had now been reached, and that Plan Orient, the "Great Plan" of driving the British out of the Middle East was at hand. Operation *Herkules* was postponed.

Operation *Herkules* is discussed in the Kesselring *Memoirs* [260], and B.H. Liddell Hart's, *The German Generals Talk* [289]. In *The Right of the Line* [461], John Terraine asserts that "Rommel would rue the day that this opportunity [to seize Malta] was lost."

EGYPT

Crossroads of the world's land routes, and a main link to the British Empire in the East, Egypt played a pivotal role during World War II. One-twelfth of Britain's oil supplies came through Egypt by way of the Suez Canal from the Persian Gulf oil fields. An independent country in which the British enjoyed "squatters' rights"--- the British fleet, army, and air force were based in that country---Egypt remained technically neutral during World War II. More than once, however, King Farouk of Egypt was compelled by the British to dismiss a prime minister who took this neutrality too seriously. The British spent 500 million pounds in Egypt during the war.

A former participant, James Lucas described what what Cairo meant for the British soldier in his book, *War in the Desert: The Eighth Army at El Alamein* [296]. To the frontline soldiers, the mass of British staff officers comfortably established in Cairo were known as "Cairo Canaries," or "Groppi Light Horse," or as "The Gabardine Swine." In Cairo, liquor was cheap and plentiful; at the front a soldier might receive a bottle of beer a month! Groppi's, an elegant cafe in Cairo and a popular meeting place for officers, was largely off-limits to "other ranks." According to Lucas, the arrival of the puritan-minded Montgomery changed the social life of Cairo; he ordered physical training for all ranks. Suddenly, it ceased to be a cheery war for many gabardine dressed Cairo staff officers.

Alexandria, port for the British Mediterranean fleet, provided another contrast with the desert war, just a few hours away. In Alexandria the war disappeared completely: hot baths, ice-cold beer, and attractive, well-dressed women made the war seem remote indeed.

In her essay, "Cairo: Back from the Blue," in *Alamein and the Desert War* [245], author Olivia Manning comments on the attitude of Egyptians toward the British: "The war was not their war; we had dragged them into it and now we looked liked losing it." Manning remarks, "Egyptians could have behaved a great deal worse."

The Egyptian political scene is discussed by Barrie St. Claire McBride in his biography, *Farouk of Egypt* [325]. On February 4, 1942, there was a demonstration against the British in Cairo, and the cry went up: "Rommel! Rommel!" The British Ambassador, with an armed escort, sealed off Farouk's palace and demanded he change the government or lose the throne.

The perspective of an Egyptian nationalist can be found in the personal reminiscence, *Revolt on the Nile* [409], by Anwar Sadat who recalled how as a young Egyptian army officer he planned to join up with Axis forces and overthrow the British. Sadat was caught by the British with two of Rommel's agents. The German spy mission, codenamed *Kondor*, is the subject of Leonard Mosley's book, *The Cat and the Mice* [346].

4

The Axis Powers in North Africa

> But it was in North Africa that a really great opportunity was missed owing to the failure of our highest authorities to appreciate the strategic possibilities of the African theater.
>
> Rommel, *The Rommel Papers*

PLAN "ORIENT," THE "GREAT PLAN"

Of all the strategic "what ifs" of World War II, perhaps none is more tantalizing than the assertion that if only Hitler had fully supported Rommel in his drive to the Middle East and its oil fields, he could have won the war. Rommel's own views are found in *The Rommel Papers* [290] edited by B.H. Liddell Hart. While an essential source, material not favorable to Rommel was left out. *The Rommel Papers* are like the sundial's motto *non numero nisi serenas* (no measurement except in fine weather).

Rommel's dream, "Plan Orient," the "Great Plan," of driving through Egypt into the Middle East, as part of a great pincer movement in which his army would link up with the Wehrmacht advancing south into the Caucasus, was no will'o-the-wisp vision in 1942. In the flush of victory following Gazala, Rommel drove his Panzerarmee eastwards at breakneck speed before the British recovered from the shock of losing Tobruk. The newly promoted Field Marshal Rommel commented, "Vielleicht kommen wir bis Kairo ("Perhaps we'll reach Cairo").

For Hitler, the decisive theater was always the East; the decisive enemy was always the Soviet Union; the decisive objective was always lebensraum. Only sporadically did Hitler accept the dream of "Plan Orient" with a triumphant German army marching into the Middle East. However, to permit the collapse of Mussolini's North African Empire was unthinkable, and in February 1941, Hitler sent over the first elements of the Afrika Korps under his tried and trusted general, Erwin Rommel. An excellent study of Hitler's thinking in regard to the Mediterranean is Walter Ansel's 1972 analysis, *Hitler and the Middle Sea* [8]. A retired rear admiral in the U.S. Navy who served in the Mediterranean theater during World War II, Ansel produced a thorough and readable account.

The post-war memoirs of German generals are a valuable source of information for the student of history, but they must be used with extreme caution since they are all too often self-serving in nature. As with any memoir, the writer may have an axe to grind, an old score to settle, or a strong reason to distort the historical record.

The most persistent advocate of a Mediterranean strategy was Admiral Erich Raeder. In his memoir, *My Life* [388], Raeder makes clear his preference for a Mediterranean strategy---"We should concentrate all our efforts on beating England, the soul of the resistance." The Admiral commented that Hitler never seemed deeply interested in attacking Malta or in other phases of the Mediterranean campaign.

In *The Memoirs of Field-Marshal Kesselring* [260], Kesselring agreed with Raeder that Hitler missed an opportunity to strike a mortal blow at England in a part of the world "vital for her." Despite self-justification and apologetics, Kesselring's memoirs are a basic source of information on World War II. From late 1941 to early 1945, he was German commander in chief in the Mediterranean area. Kesselring made it obvious that he had continuous differences with Rommel. Regarding those differences, historian Gerhard Weinberg points out in his tour de force *A World At Arms: A Global History of World War II* [487], that they were much less successful at working things out than American and British commanders. Despite the title, Kenneth Macksey's study, *Kesselring: The Making of the Luftwaffe* [309], focused on Kesselring's role as commander in chief of German forces in the Mediterranean theater.

The German General Staff viewed "Plan Orient" with cynicism. Rommel's "African adventure" is treated skeptically in *The Halder Diaries* [141] edited in the English language edition by T.N. Dupuy. General Franz Halder was Chief of the German General Staff. Halder thought Rommel "pathologically ambitious" and "in no way equal to the task." He asked on one occasion, has "This General [Rommel] gone raving mad!"

The views of the German General Staff (OKH) are often mentioned in *The German Generals Talk* [289] by B.H. Liddell Hart. Other recollections by German generals are General Walter Warlimont, *Inside Hitler's Headquarters* [482], and General Siegfried Westphal's essay in *The Fatal Decisions* [167] edited by Seymour Freidin.

Among post-war writers, Kurt Assman in his book *Deutsche Schicksahlsjahre* [10], claimed that a decisive German commitment to the North African theater in 1940 or 1941, would have won the war. That view was rejected by Andreas Hillgruber in his study, *Hitler's Strategie, Politik, Kriegfuhrung* [212], who insisted that Hitler was right in refusing to regard North Africa as anything but a secondary theater.

Hitler's strategic decisions were assessed by Ronald Lewin in his book, *Hitler's Mistakes* [283]. Lewin criticized Hitler's "failure of vision," unlike Admiral Raeder who had the "percipience" to grasp the strategic value of the Mediterranean. In the book's introduction, historian Stephen E. Ambrose wrote a touching reminiscence of Lewin who is remembered for his fair-minded studies of Wavell, Montgomery and Rommel, and who died shortly after completing his last book, *Hitler's Mistakes*, in 1984.

The "What if?" question was addressed by Martin van Creveld in his readable study, *Supplying War: Logistics from Wallenstein to Patton* [475]. Van Creveld offered a fresh view from the logistic angle, often neglected. Van Creveld attempted to demonstrate that the Germans never had the logistic capability adequately to reinforce the Egyptian front, and that it was therefore pointless to theorize about the degree of decisiveness of a non-existent alternative.

AFRIKA KORPS

From a small force sent to support the Italians and block any British advance beyond western Libya, the Afrika Korps became a legend under its commander Erwin Rommel. Official German sources on the operations of the Afrika Korps include Charles Burdick's, *Unternehmen Sonnenblume* [66], volume 48 in the Wehrmacht im Kampf series, and *Der Mittelmeerraum und Sudosteuropa* (The Mediterranean, Southeast Europe, and North Africa, 1939-1941) [419] by Gerhard Schreiber, Bernd Stegemann, and Detlef Vogel. The English language edition was published in 1992. The volume is part of the ongoing series, "Das Deutsche Reich und der Zweite Weltkrieg" (Germany in World War II). In the opinion of historian Gerhard L. Weinberg, the section on the North African campaigns by Bernd Stegemann offers the best account of the events surrounding Rommel's first victories and defeats in the desert.

General F.W. Von Mellenthin's book, *Panzer Battles: A Study of the Employment of Armor in the Second World War* [478], is a classic study of the tactics, planning, and operations of the Afrika Korps. Von Mellenthin was Rommel's extraordinarily efficient intelligence officer.

Paul Carell, the pseudonym of a German journalist who served as an Intelligence officer in North Africa, authored *The Foxes of the Desert* [72]. Carell received "advice and help" from several former generals. His research included conversations with more than a thousand veterans who served in the Afrika Korps. Carell brings out the humor of the German soldier, as well as his combative spirit. Less successful is the constant attempt to excuse the defeats of the Afrika Korps by blaming Hitler, the lack of supplies, and the Italians.

Exceptionally well-written is the 1989 memoir by Hans von Luck, *Panzer Commander: The Memoirs of Colonel Hans von Luck* [301]. In his introduction, Stephen E. Ambrose called it "simply superb," "an instant classic," and noted that apart from von Luck himself, the dominant personality in the memoir was Erwin Rommel. The author was a respected and valued protégé of Rommel, first as a military student studying tactics and later primarily as a reconnaissance battalion commander serving under him in several campaigns. Von Luck showed in his memoir the finest face of the old Prussian officer class. He mentions several instances of where both sides "fought clean" in the North African war.

Other German accounts include Volkmar Kuhn's, *Rommel in the Desert: Victories and Defeat of the Afrika-Korps, 1941-1943* [275]; Hanns-Gert von Esebeck's, *Das Deutsche Afrika-Korps* [149], and Walter Nehring's, *Die Deutsche Panzerwaffe, 1916-45* [350]. Nehring commanded the Afrika Korps under Rommel from May to August 1942.

In 1968, Ronald Lewin wrote *Rommel as Military Commander*, followed three years later by *Montgomery as Military Commander*. To complete the trilogy, in 1977

there appeared Lewin's *Life and Death of the Afrika Korps* [284]. He tells the story
of the *Deutsches Afrika Korps* as seen by the Germans themselves and what they
thought of their enemies. Lewin showed that the Afrika Korps fought each battle with
a preconceived tactical doctrine designed by Rommel to suit the desert. The
formations that made up the famed *D.A.K.* consisted of the 15th Panzer Division, the
21st Panzer Division, and the 90th Light Division.

A highly readable account by a British desert veteran is *Panzer Army Afrika* [297]
by James Lucas. Lucas made extensive use of German sources and interviews with
Afrika Korps veterans. He covers such topics as food, hygiene, and tactics.

The story of "Lilli Marlene," the most famous song to emerge from the desert war
is told by Derek Jewell in *Alamein and the Desert War* [245]. First beamed to the
German troops in Africa from Radio Belgrade in August 1941, "Lilli Marlene" became
a fixture on Radio Belgrade at 9:55 pm, the last record of the night. Singer Lale
Andersen received an estimated one million letters from German soldiers.

Originally published in France, *The Afrika Korps* [33], by Erwan Bergot is an
admiring account of Rommel and his "corps d'elite." Kenneth Macksey's *Afrika Korps*
[306] was an excellent contribution to Ballentine's Illustrated history of World War
II; A.J. Barker, *Afrika Korps* [20] and George Forty, *Afrika Korps: The Long Road
Back* [161] are useful contributions.

ROMMEL

In the British House of Commons in November 1941, Winston Churchill told the
members, "We have a very daring and skillful opponent against us, and, may I say
across the havoc of war, a great general." In the aftermath of the disastrous British
defeat at Gazala in June 1942, Churchill would say, striding up and down late at night,
"Rommel, Rommel, Rommel, Rommel! What else matters but beating him?"
Churchill's volume *The Hinge of Fate* [92] describes the crisis when Rommel and his
Axis forces came within an ace of driving all the way to the Nile.

Of all the superstars of Twentieth Century warfare, perhaps none shines brighter
than Rommel. In a book review for *The Journal of Military History* [349],
Williamson Murray called Rommel "undoubtedly the greatest battlefield general of the
war." Stephen E. Ambrose and other military historians have ranked Rommel as the
best general of World War II. From simulated war games to videocassettes, Rommel
has received remarkable attention; in the BBC-Time Life television series the
"Commanders," the script for *Erwin Rommel-Field Marshal of the German Army*
[404] was written by Correlli Barnett.

In addition to *The Rommel Papers* a close-up view of the general known as the
Desert Fox is found in the account *The German Army in the West* [490] written by his
Chief of Staff Siegfried Westphal who called Rommel "not only the soul but also the
motive power of the North African war." Westphal described both his strengths and
weaknesses, successfully communicating Rommel's driving energy as he swoops down
in his "Stork" to drop a message to the commander below: "If you do not move on at
once, I shall come down. Rommel."

Another account written by a member of Rommel's staff was that by F.W. von Mellenthin, *Panzer Battles* [478]. When asked what he thought of James Mason's portrayal of Rommel in the 1951 film *The Desert Fox*, Rommel's former Intelligence Officer smiled and said, "Altogether too polite." The motion picture was based on the biography by Desmond Young, *Rommel: The Desert Fox* [500]. Young's book was the first English language biography of Rommel. The author had been captured in North Africa, and he briefly encountered Rommel who took his side in a dispute with a German officer. Adulatory in tone, Young's biography launched the literary legend of Rommel.

Ronald Lewin's 1968 study, *Rommel as Military Commander* [286], neither glamorized nor canonized his subject, but viewed Rommel as much more than an ordinary German general. A participant in the desert war himself, Lewin gives his narrative the whiff of battle.

In his essay, "Rommel Reassessed," in *Alamein and the Desert War* [245], German historian Hans-Adolf Jacobsen claimed that Rommel was basically a dashing divisional commander, and not much more. In his memoir, *A Don at War* [229], David Hunt charged that Rommel was merely "a dashing cavalryman who gambled deep and lost in the end." The author served as an Intelligence officer on General Sir Harold Alexander's staff in North Africa.

With the publication of David Irving's 1977 biography, *On the Trail of the Fox* [233], the reader was offered a more life-like portrait of Rommel than any previous work. Based on an extraordinary array of new sources---correspondence, diaries, and personal testimony of survivors of the period---Irving showed that Rommel could be overbearing, obstinate, sometimes petty, avid for decorations and acclaim. Despite what might be termed these minor character flaws, Irving waxes lyrical about Rommel's military genius, bestowing on him the ultimate accolade---that of a 20th Hannibal. To Irving, the British won or Rommel lost only because of *Ultra*. More descriptive than analytical, Irving regales the reader with Rommel's chivalry, bravery, and personal magnetism. Ronald Lewin, in a review of Irving's book, concluded that Rommel still "scintillates: a bright particular star." Reviewer David Pryce-Jones, however, observed that in Irving's biography Rommel and Nazism are pure and shining, their cause only tainted by a few degenerates.

Irving's book should be used with caution suggested Rommel's trusted friend Admiral Friedrich Ruge in "The Trail of the Fox: A Comment," *Military Affairs* [408].

A military reappraisal of Rommel is offered by Wolf Heckmann in his book, *Rommel's War in Africa* [204], published in 1981. The author served in the German army at the end of World War II when he was sixteen. Heckmann is highly critical of Rommel, claiming that his victories owed more to the superiority of German weapons than to the superiority of his generalship. In the book's foreword, General Sir John Hackett is much more generous in his assessment of Rommel, among other things commenting that no general was more willingly followed by his troops. In 1987, *Das Fuhrers General* [395], by Ralf Reuth was published in Germany.

The most recent biography of Rommel, *Knight's Cross: A Life of Field Marshal Erwin Rommel* [166], is that written by British General Sir David Fraser which was published in 1993. Essentially a military biography, Fraser provides an expert analysis of Rommel's military ability. The figure that emerges is the Rommel of legend: straightforward, honest, a tactical genius, and a naive patriot who had little doubt about the justness of Germany's cause. To quote historian Richard Overy's *Times Literary Supplement* [361] review, Rommel's image as a "squeaky-clean general" lingers on.

A stimulating discussion of Rommel and logistics is found in Martin van Creveld's book, *Supplying War* [474]; Also useful are John Ellis's *Brute Force* [145], and Martin Cooper's *The German Army 1933-45: Its Political and Military Failure* [111]. Cooper quotes Rommel's famous remark to Halder, "That's quite immaterial to me [supply]. That's your pigeon." Among the legion of other sources on Rommel are Warren Tute's, *The North African War* [462], with a foreword by Rommel's son, Manfred; Kenneth Macksey's, *Rommel: Battles and Campaigns* [310]; Richard L. Blanco's, *The Desert Warrior: The Afrika Korps in World War II* [43]; Samuel W. Mitcham, Jr., *Triumphant Fox: Erwin Rommel and the Rise of the Afrika Korps* [334]; and Jack Greene and Alessandro Massignani, *Rommel's North African Campaign: September 1940-November 1942* [189].

NORTH AFRICA: AN ITALIAN THEATER OF WAR

The story of Italy's war in North Africa is slowly emerging out of the shadow cast by Rommel and the Afrika Korps. At all times the majority of Rommel's troops were Italian. At no time did he have more than five German divisions under his command. In North Africa, Rommel was under an Italian superior officer until February 1943--- although he often disregarded the orders of his Italian and German superiors. Libya, an Italian colony, was the responsibility of Italian General Italo Gariboldi who in turn was under the command of the Italian High Command in Rome, the *Comando Supremo*. Unlike the Americans and British, there was no Combined Chiefs of Staff organization between the Germans and Italians to integrate Axis strategy. If the Allies had difficulties working together, they were minimal when compared to those of the Axis powers. Hitler and Mussolini preferred to direct their war efforts entirely independent of each other.

The Italian perspective can be found in the diary of Marshal Ugo Cavallero, *Comando Supremo. Diario 1940-1943* [82]. Cavallero was head of the *Comando Supremo*. The diary of Mussolini's Foreign Secretary (and son in law) is also useful, *The Ciano Diaries* [93].

THE ITALIAN ARMY AND AIR FORCE

In 1940 Mussolini had good reason to think that the Italian Army chief of staff, Marshal Pietro Badoglio (who became head of the Italian government in 1943 after Il Duce's overthrow), was correct in thinking that an offensive against the British in Egypt would be "easy and foolproof." Badoglio's memoirs first appeared in Italian in 1946 and have been translated into English under the title, *Italy in the Second World War* [16]. Italy's armored forces on the eve of war are analyzed in *Iron Arm: The*

Mechanization of Mussolini's Army, 1920-1940 [453] by John J.T. Sweet. In terms of vehicles and manpower, Italy was the Axis power with the greatest number of armored forces committed to the war in North Africa in 1940-1942. A total of 167,000 Italian and Italian colonial troops in Libya faced 36,000 British, Indians, and New Zealanders in Egypt. Over 1,000 Italian combat aircraft faced three biplane fighters on Malta and 200 largely obsolete British aircraft based in Egypt. At sea, the Italians were numerically superior in cruisers, destroyers, submarines, and light units. Mussolini, who had repeatedly spoken of possessing "eight million steelhearted fighters," boasted that "our boys will pass, over mountains of bodies." The subsequent inglorious collapse of Graziani's army at the hands of O'Connor and Wavell would cast a long shadow over the performance of the Italian armed forces. While noting individual exceptions, German generals were usually critical of the Italian combat performance: In *The Memoirs of Field-Marshal Kesselring* [260], Albert Kesselring comments that Italians were "trained more for display than for action." A more generous assessment is made by F.W. von Mellenthin in his memoir, *Panzer Battles* [478].

In his study, *A Time for Courage* [461], John Terraine states that one British Hurricane fighter attached to the Western Desert Air Force in 1940, served as an effective deterrent in support of the outclassed Gladiators. By seizing the initiative and acting aggressively at the very beginning of the war, Terraine claims that the RAF gained complete moral ascendancy over the Italians. Despite many brave individual pilots and crews and some useful aircraft, the *Regia Aeronautica* or Italian air force, was no more than "a fringe activity in the march of war."

In his essay, "The Sources of Italy's Defeat in 1940: Bluff or Institutionalized Incompetence?" which appeared in the volume, *German Nationalism and the European Response, 1890-1945* [158], historian MacGregor Knox concluded that institutionalized incompetence was the primary villain. Knox cites the alleged comment of General Ubaldo Soddu to one of his staff, "when you have a fine plate of pasta guaranteed for life, and a little music, you don't need anything more." The author based his research on the official Italian histories of the war, and on memoirs of Italian generals and admirals.

MacGregor Knox authored the essay, "The Italian Armed Forces," for volume III of the study *Military Effectiveness* [332], which was edited by Allan R. Millet and Williamson Murray. Knox pillories the Italian military for its rigidity and refusal to change in the face of defeat after defeat. He attributes its "intellectual parochialism" and "nationalist arrogance" to Fascism. Knox's work, *Mussolini Unleashed, 1939-1941: Politics and Strategy in Fascist Italy's Last War* [271], contains an extensive bibliography listing many Italian-language sources. Italy's military performance is addressed in John Gooch's article, "Italian Military Competence," *The Journal of Strategic Studies* [184].

For over 40 years, Italian historian Lucio Ceva contributed to the literature on the Italian war in North Africa. His study, *La Condotta Italiana Della Guerra. Cavallero e il Comando Supremo* [85], is an indispensable monograph on the Italian high command in World War II. Published in 1982, *Africa Settentrionale 1940-1943* [84], is a collection of essays that summarizes Ceva's lifetime of writing on the subject of the Italian war in North Africa. His article, "The North African Campaign 1940-43: A Reconsideration," was translated by John Gooch and appeared in *The Journal of Strategic Studies* [83]. A version of the essay is found in *Decisive Campaigns of the Second World War* [183], edited by Gooch. Ceva rejects the common assumption that the Italians fought poorly because their hearts were not in the war. He suggests that Italian hearts were not in the war, but that the armored divisions, *Ariete* and *Trieste*, along with the German-trained paratroops of the *Folgore* division, fought well. According to Ceva, these units were no more enthusiastic about the war than those that fought poorly. What made the difference was proper leadership, combat experience, and the German example.

Charging that "Anglo-Saxon racism" permeates the historiography, revisionist historian James J. Sadkovich argued in his essay, "German Military Incompetence Through Italian Eyes," published in 1994 in the journal *War in History*, that Anglo-American historians have tended to reflect the German rather than the Italian point of view. Sadkovich rejects the view that the Germans were the more competent of the two allies; instead, the Germans are portrayed as the more "cautious," "timid," "careless," and "inept" Axis partner.

The quality of the Italian army is briefly discussed by John Ellis in his work, *Brute Force* [145]. One weakness of that army cited by Ellis was the lack of trained NCOs. In June 1940, the ratio of NCOs to private soldiers in the Italian army was 1:33. In the American army in 1945, the ratio was 1:2. The result was inadequate combat training. Mussolini's new legions, declares Ellis, were about as ineffective on the modern battlefield as those of Scipio Africanus.

Of the 500,000 Italian soldiers captured by the Allies in North Africa and later Sicily, 50,000 were transferred to the United States as POWs. Louis E. Keefer's book, *Italian Prisoners of War in America 1942-1946* [253], offers an interesting account of their experiences.

THE ITALIAN NAVY AND *ULTRA*

The Italy navy, historiography, and *Ultra* were addressed in a paper delivered by Italian naval historian Alberto Santoni before the Tenth Naval History Symposium held at the U.S. Naval Academy in Annapolis, Maryland, in 1991. Under the title, "The Italian Navy at the Outbreak of World War II and the Influence of British *Ultra* Intelligence on Mediterranean Operations," Professor Santoni's paper was published in the volume *New Interpretations in Naval History* published by the Naval Institute Press and edited by Jack Sweetman.

Santoni frankly describes much of Italian writing on World War II as "extremely shortsighted" and "lacking in objectivity," owing in many cases to conflict between pro-fascist and anti-fascist viewpoints. Santoni remarks that the first Italian account of Mediterranean operations by Marc'Antonio Bragadin, a naval officer during the war, did not add to the prestige of Italian scholarship. The book was published in translation by the U.S. Naval Institute in 1957 under the title, *The Italian Navy in World War II* [56]. Bragadin used the terms "magnificent" and "above reproach" to refer to Italian morale, and attributed all sinkings of British ships in the Mediterranean to Italian forces, failing to mention the large German military presence in the theater. Santoni observed that during the entire war Italian naval gunnery managed to sink only two craft, and those were British motor torpedoboats.

Santoni also criticizes certain Italian memoirs for being unreliable sources, specifically citing the books of Admiral Angelo Iachino, the commander in chief of the Italian fleet between 1940 and 1943.

There are 23 volumes of the official series *La Marina Italiana nella Seconda Guerra Mondiale* (The Italian Navy in the Second World War), that have been published by the Historical Department of the Italian navy since 1959. Santoni comments that in light of *Ultra* intelligence revelations, the Historical Department has made the decision to rewrite the most important volumes in the Italian naval series.

Santoni made his own contribution to the literature on Intelligence with the publication of his book, *Il Vero Traditore: Il Ruolo Documentato di Ultra nella Guerra del Mediterraneo*. Beginning in June 1941, *Ultra* codebreakers at Bletchley Park, managed to monitor the movements of Italian convoys crossing to Libya, accurately revealing their timetables, ports of departure and arrival, speeds, routes, and escorts. All of this information was due to the detailed information the Italians had to send by radio to the Libyan ports to make it possible for the incoming convoys to be unloaded as quickly as possible. Both Santoni and Ralph Bennett (*Ultra and Mediterranean Strategy* [32]), note the strict measures that the British took to conceal *Ultra*. There always had to be a sighting by an aircraft on an apparently routine patrol over the area before any air or surface attack. Even so, Italian covoys were attacked so often that Rome (and the Germans) suspected that there were traitors inside the Italian navy.

THE MORALE QUESTION

In his book, *Red Duster, White Ensign: The Story of the Malta Convoys* [70], Ian Cameron had little patience with those accounts which dismissed the Italian sailors as "arrant cowards." He remarked that such comments unintentionally belittled the exploits of whose who fought against them. Cameron praises the courage and daring of the Italian crewmen of the human-torpedoes that badly damaged the two British battleships *Valiant* and *Queen Elizabeth* in Alexandria harbor in December 1941. He asserts that some squadrons of the *Regia Aeronautica* pressed home their attacks far more bravely and skilfully than any German unit, with the exception of Fliegerkorps X.

The question of fighting spirit in the Italian navy is addressed by French Admiral Raymond De Belot, in his survey, *The Struggle for the Mediterranean 1939-1945* [128]. He believes that Allied propaganda created the false impression that the Royal Navy won an easy victory in the Mediterranean. He claims that British successes at Taranto (three Italian battleships heavily damaged) and Matapan (three Italian cruisers sunk) were exaggerated by propaganda. While recognizing the cautious and defensive attitude of the Italian naval high command, De Belot rejects the notion that Italian sailors lacked fighting spirit.

An American naval officer W.D. Puleston, in his account, *The Influence of Sea Power* [387], attributed the British navy's success in the Mediterranean to the superiority of its personnel. While a few Italian naval officers displayed remarkable courage and skill, Puleston claims that most showed no desire for close combat with the enemy.

The *Historical Dictionary of Fascist Italy* [71], edited by Philip V. Cannistraro, contains several contributions by MacGregor Knox. Knox's contribution on the Battle of Matapan asserts that the engagement confirmed the Italian naval leadership's inferiority complex vis-à-vis the British. A detailed treatment of the battle is that by British naval writer S.W.C. Pack, *The Battle of Matapan* [364].

Revisionist historian James J. Sadkovich has argued in articles and monographs that the Italian combat performance in the Mediterranean and North Africa has been grossly underestimated. He edited and contributed to the book, *Reevaluating Major Naval Combatants of World War II* [410]. His article, "Re-evaluating Who Won the Italo-British Naval Conflict, 1940-2," *European History Quarterly* [411], concluded that the combat performance of the Royal Navy was not appreciably different from that of the *Regia Marina*, and that the naval struggle was "a draw rather than a convincing win for either side."

Sadkovich expanded upon his revisionist views in his study, *The Italian Navy in World War II* [412]. Rejecting what he terms the "myths" surrounding the World War II performance of the *Regia Marina*, Sadkovich attributes Italian defeats to the British possession of *Ultra*, radar, and "luck"; he asserts that British success at Taranto "owed something to a storm" that tore loose barrage balloons protecting the Italian battleships.

If Sadkovich sometimes overstates his case and overpraises the *Regia Marina*, his work is a useful corrective to the World War II joke that American sailors like whiskey, British sailors prefer rum, but Italian sailors stick to port! Italian mines and torpedoes sank 132 British warships in the Mediterranean or 56 per cent of all Royal Navy vessels in that theater.

An important source on Axis naval operations in the Mediterranean is the study by Walter Baum and Eberhard Weichold, *Der Krieg der "Achsenmächte" im Mittelmeer-Raum: Die "Strategie" der Diktatoren* [25]. Weichold was the "German Admiral in Rome" from June 1940 to March 1943, serving as senior liaison officer to the Italy Naval Staff and, after November 1941, also had command of German naval operations in the Mediterranean.

THE AXIS ON FILM

In his study, *The American World War II Film* [134], Bernard F. Dick claims that the Italians were impossible to dislike even when they were Allied with Hitler. In the movies, Hollywood never treated Italy as an enemy, preferring to focus hostility on the dictator Mussolini. That six Italian divisions fought with Rommel made little difference; the Italians in the desert war were either harmless, like the general in *Five Graves to Cairo* (1943), or expressed regret over what had happened like Giuseppe in *Sahara* (1943) who begs not to be judged by his insignia: "Only the body wears the uniform."

A helpful analysis of Hollywood wartime film productions is Robert Fyne's, *The Hollywood Propaganda of World War II* [173]. In the 1943 film *Sahara*, Humphrey Bogart starred as a tough-talking tank commander who leads a motley group of Allied soldiers across the desert. *Sahara* was listed as one of the ten best films of the war.

Five Graves to Cairo, in which Rommel was played by the former Austrian actor Erich von Stroheim. Rommel is caricatured as an aristocratic Nazi officer easily fooled by a cockamamie story. For sheer escapism there was the movie, *Tarzan's Desert Victory*, in which the Ape Man (Johnny Weissmuller) routs the Germans in the Sahara. Besides succinct descriptions, Fyne's account includes a useful chronological list of Hollywood propaganda films from 1941 to 1945.

5

Montgomery, Alam Halfa, and El Alamein

Here we will stand and fight; there will be no further withdrawal. If we can't stay here alive, then let us stay here dead.

Montgomery, *Memoirs*

A NEW BROOM

A mere ten days after the capture of Tobruk, Axis forces were only 60 miles from Alexandria. Already, Hitler and Mussolini had decided that Rommel would command the Army of Occupation in Egypt. In Tripoli, Mussolini prepared to ride his white stallion in triumph into Cairo. One more bold effort, and Rommel would be on the banks of the Nile. A turning point in North African war was close at hand.

Winston Churchill's *The Hinge of Fate* [92], and *The Alanbrooke War Diaries* [64], edited by Arthur Bryant, provide information on British decision making at the highest level. General Sir Alan Brooke (later Viscount Alanbrooke) was Churchill's Chief of the Imperial General Staff. General W.H.E. "Strafer" Gott was first choice to command the 8th Army, but when he was killed, Montgomery was appointed to take his place.

Montgomery's own account of his first few hours and days in the desert, perhaps the most important in his military life, appear in *The Memoirs of Field Marshal The Viscount Montgomery of Alamein* [337]. According to his biographer, Nigel Hamilton, "The Memoirs" are "the most controversial military autobiography of the century." The initial title had been *The Sparks Fly Upward*, and that was no misnomer. The writing of "The Memoirs" is discussed in the third and final volume of Hamilton's monumental biography *Monty* [199]. No other passage in the memoirs caused more uproar in Britain than the claim that Auchinleck's intended to withdraw from the Alamein line before Montgomery took command. Battle lines were drawn between the two distinguished field-marshals and their respective champions. While Montgomery never retracted his statement concerning Auchinleck's intention to withdraw, he did eventually acknowledge Auchinleck's contribution to stabilizing the Alamein front before his arrival in the desert.

· Montgomery's memoirs are an indispensable primary source on the War in North Africa, as well as revealing a good deal about the personality of the author. Sometimes misleading and disingenious, they are at other times refreshingly outspoken and candid. His only too obvious flaws brought him bitter enemies and distressed his friends. For the sake of fairness and historical accuracy, corroboration from other sources is absolutely necessary.

Montgomery took command of the 8th Army at 1400 hours on August 13, 1942, two days before he had been authorized to do so. He found the desert headquarters of the 8th Army "dismal," "dreary," "unreal," and "dangerous." His memoirs describe the dramatic scene when he first spoke to his headquarters staff the evening of his arrival. Declaring there would be no more withdrawals, Montgomery told his officers that the 8th Army would do the same, if need be, as the ancient Spartans had done defending to the death the pass at Thermopylae. After his speech, wrote Montgomery, "One could have heard a pin drop if such a thing was possible in the sand of the desert!"

Among those present at the staff meeting was Francis de Guingand who became Montgomery's Chief of Staff and later wrote his memoir, *Operation Victory* [129]. De Guingand's comments are particularly important since he had previously served as Auchinleck's Chief of Staff and liked him very much. De Guingand described Montgomery's evening talk to the 8th Army's staff officers as "electric," "terrific," and "cool as a refreshing breeze." With his unequivocal order that there would be no withdrawal, no doubters, no "bellyaching," Montgomery created a new spirit in the 8th Army.

General Bernard Freyburg who commanded the 2nd New Zealand Division, would say later that the arrival of Alexander and Montgomery in the Middle East marked the end of his three unhappiest years. Freyburg is the subject of an essay by Dan Davin in *The War Lords* [76] edited by Michael Carver.

Montgomery's impact on the 8th Army is mentioned by Michael Carver in his biography, *Harding of Petherton* [79]. Harding (a future Field Marshal) was one of the young new commanders appointed by Montgomery. He was given command of the oldest of all the desert formations, the 7th Armored Division, "the Desert Rats."

In *The Causes of Wars and Other Essays* [223], Michael Howard comments that whether or not Auchinleck planned to withdraw from El Alamein to another defensive line, the uncertainty ended with the arrival of Montgomery who ordered all transport back to Cairo. Withdrawal was no longer an option.

ALAM HALFA

Once thought likely to jeopardize Montgomery's military reputation more than that of any other Allied commander, the *Ultra* revelations have not done so. Instead, they have illuminated both his strengths and weaknesses, as well as putting to rest some venerable controversies in the historical literature. In his review essay, "Ralph Bennett and the Study of Ultra," *Intelligence and National Security* [155], John Ferris declared that Bennett's *Ultra and Mediterranean Strategy* [32] "nails shut the coffin which encloses the earthly remains of *The Desert Generals*, R.I.P." Ferris remarked that Bennett avoids the problem of personality cults which have traditionally dogged the literature: his Montgomery is neither Wellington returned nor an imposter unmasked."

In *Ultra and Mediterranean Strategy*, Bennet rejects the claim of Auchinleck advocates that the July 1942 battles were "The First Alamein." Based on *Ultra* decrypts of German radio signals, the evidence corroborates the view that Rommel "ran out of steam" in July rather supporting the thesis of Auchinleck's proponents that he had won a "decisive" battle. Bennett declared that the erroneously termed "First Alamein" was no more than a "temporary check.".

Besides resolving the venerable controversy over the July battles, Bennett put another long contentious issue to rest, namely what if any credit did Montgomery owe Auchinleck for the plans that led to his first successful battle at Alam Halfa. The official British history of Intelligence by F.H. Hinsley, *British Intelligence in the Second World War: Its Influence on Strategy and Operations, Vol. II* [215], claimed that "No basic change was made to Eighth Army's plans following the change of commander." Ralph Bennett minces no words when he charges that Hinsley "mischievously mishandles evidence" when he implies that Montgomery took over Auchinleck's plan.

On the day of his arrival at the front, August 13, Montgomery reconnoitered the Alam Halfa area and immediately sensed the supreme importance of holding the Alam Halfa ridge on the left rear of the British line. Bennett comments that Auchinleck's defensive arrangements (written by Dorman-Smith) had not provided a strong garrison for the ridge, nor did Auchinleck provide one in his last few days as 8th Army commander. What is certain, declares Bennett, is that Montgomery "appreciated at once that the Alam Halfa ridge was of vital importance, but was virtually undefended." At 2200 hours on the evening of August 13, Montgomery asked for and got the 44th Division from General Alexander (Command-in-Chief Middle East) to garrison the ridge. Montgomery's summons for the 44th Division went out only twelve hours after he had arrived at 8th Army headquarters.

Rommel had previously spotted Alam Halfa ridge as the key to the whole El Alamein position. On August 15 (two days after Montgomery's decision), Rommel informed Berlin that he planned to attack in the south. By intercepting and decrypting Rommel's signal, *Ultra* confirmed that Montgomery's military instinct was right. Rommel attacked on August 30, and on September 6 Axis armor turned back with nothing to show for its efforts but burned-out tanks; Alam Halfa, declares Bennett, was the turning-point in the African campaign and the first unequivocal victory of a British general over Rommel.

At Alam Halfa, for the first time, a coolly calculating commander had checked the "cavalry instinct" of the armored forces from charging after Rommel and into a possible concentrated firepower trap. Montgomery wasted no time reorganizing, reequipping, and retraining his forces after Alam Halfa. Under pressure from Churchill to attack, Montgomery was adamant that he would only attack when ready and not before. He got his way. By October, Montgomery deployed eleven divisions, four of which were armored divisions with a total of just over 1,000 tanks, among them 250 Shermans, supported by 900 guns and 530 aircraft.

THE BATTLE OF EL ALAMEIN (OCTOBER 23-NOVEMBER 4, 1942)

A vast literature and much mythology have grown up around the Battle of El Alamein and the preceeding crucial summer months of 1942. On the twentieth anniversary of the battle, two accounts were published by authors who fought there: Michael Carver's expert study, *El Alamein* [78] and Lucas Phillips lively narrative, *Alamein* [375]. Both books have stood the test of time and become standard works on the subject. Both authors dealt convincingly with critics who insisted that Montgomery could have destroyed Rommel at Alam Halfa, hence El Alamein was a costly and unnecessary battle. Both Carver and Phillips showed that El Alamein, like Waterloo, was "a damned [near] thing." Rather than any material superiority, Carver argued that Montgomery's speed and clarity of thought were the deciding factor in the battle's outcome. His reliable narrative is "tinged with the residual passion of one who participated."

Lucas Phillips presented the battle from the soldier's point of view, obtaining much of his evidence from interviews with a large number of survivors. Phillips noted that Rommel's reputation was dangerously high among British troops before El Alamein. Although Phillips was a strong Montgomery fan, he did not make the mistake of suggesting that the 8th Army was a dispirited and disorganized rabble which sprang to life only with the arrival of Montgomery.

An excellent short account of the battle is Fred Majdalany's, *The Battle of El Alamein: Fortress in the Sand* [312], which was published in 1965. His assessment of Montgomery: "At a moment when history held its breath, he rallied his country's soldiers as Churchill had rallied its people." In the opinion of Majdalany, El Alamein transformed a "dilettante force of brave amateurs" into an army that was at last beginning to be professional and would become more so.

To commemorate the 25th Anniversary of El Alamein, the London Sunday Times newspaper invited Field Marshal Montgomery to return to Africa in 1967 and recreate the story of the battle. To Montgomery's subsequent account were added contributions by other writers and military experts: the result was published in the Ballantine War Book series under the title, *Alamein and the Desert War* [245], edited by Derek Jewell. Partly commemorative and reminiscent, and partly reassessment, the collection of essays and color photographs provide a superb overview of the war in the desert.

The 40th Anniversary of El Alamein was marked by a number of works. Author James Lucas, himself a veteran of the desert war, presented a vivid account of what living and fighting were like on the bleak, sun-scorched, limestone western desert plateau. In his book, *War in the Desert: The Eighth Army at El Alamein* [296]. Lucas reminded the reader that in 1942 El Alamein was no more than "a row of shattered shacks" and a train station 60 miles from Alexandria. The author declared that Montgomery won a clear-cut victory at an acceptable cost in casualties of 13,500, a figure almost exactly predicted by Montgomery. Lucas considered El Alamein as important as the great contemporary struggle at Stalingrad. Later generations, he remarked, have no conception of the "pride of Empire, which time has not diminished." Barrie Pitt's, *The Crucible of War: Year of Alamein 1942* [380], was the sequel to his *Western Desert 1941* [379]. A former participant in the war, Pitt's account is a workmanlike, day-to-day study of both British and German armies.

The 1981 account, *El Alamein: Desert Victory* [449], by John Strawson presented the traditional pro-Auchinleck, anti-Montgomery case. The author argued that El Alamein was not decisive and that the battle was "puny" compared to Stalingrad. He insisted that Montgomery's material superiority was so great that there was nothing remarkable about the victory. What would have been extraordinary, wrote Strawson, was if Montgomery had failed to win the battle. The author repeated the assertions of Auchinleck's partisans that he was the general who really defeated Rommel in July, and that Montgomery's battle plans at Alam Halfa and El Alamein were derived from those of Auchinleck.

The argument that Rommel faced a "hopelessly unequal struggle" at El Alamein was repeated by John Ellis in his 1990 revisionist view of World War II, *Brute Force: Allied Strategy and Tactics in the Second World War* [145]. To the author, the outcome was "never much in doubt." Ellis's argument is that the Allied victory in World War II was the inevitable consequence of their superior industrial resources, but that the war lasted longer than necessary because Allied commanders deployed their strength so clumsily. Ellis claims that Allied advantages, public relations officers, and a press hungry for heroes made generals Montgomery and Patton only "seem like great commanders." The author's viewpoint is not new, but his thesis is forcefully presented. Reviewer Carlo D'Este noted in *The Journal of Military History* [125] that Ellis relies too heavily on hindsight and not enough on the "fog of war." D'Este points out that Ellis overlooks the all-important but intangible virtues of leadership that mold armies and inspire men to fight in a place like El Alamein.

Was the Battle of El Alamein even necessary? Critics of Montgomery have argued that either he could have destroyed Rommel after Alam Halfa or that the *Torch* landings would have forced Rommel to retreat without the necessity of a battle at El Alamein.

In his study, *Montgomery as Military Commander* [265], Ronald Lewin rejected as "wholly unrealistic" the argument that El Alamein was unnecessary. Lewin asked rhetorically was Montgomery to stand idly by while Malta succumbed? Were the American supplied Sherman tanks not to be used, while Americans fought their way to Tunis from the west? Would Churchill have calmly accepted inaction? Would Hitler and Mussolini have permitted Rommel to withdraw at El Alamein?

A fair-minded evaluation of Montgomery was presented by Michael Howard (now Lord Howard) in his book, *The Causes of Wars and Other Essays* [223]. Howard's essay on Montgomery first appeared at the time of Montgomery's death in 1976. In sheer material terms, Howard accepted that Montgomery had "enormous advantages" which his predecessors lacked, such as Grants and Shermans instead of Matildas and Valentines. However, he strongly disagreed with those critics who insisted that Montgomery "could not miss" since the cards were stacked in his favor. No one in London, Cairo, the desert, or elsewhere regarded a British victory as a foregone conclusion in October 1942. There had been too many defeats---Dunkirk, Singapore, conclusion in October 1942. There had been too many defeats---Dunkirk, Singapore, Burma, Greece, Crete, and then the shattering blow of Tobruk---to speak of a foregone conclusion. In that grim summer of 1942, the world watched an almost unknown general take on the world-famous Rommel.

Montgomery's official campaign narrative, *El Alamein to the River Sangro* [336], published in 1948, presented a chronological account of the battle. The El Alamein line was one of the few times in the desert conflict where outflanking the enemy was impossible: in the north the Mediterranean, and in the south the huge sand sea of the Qattara Depression, seven hundred feet below the desert; a front of about 35 miles in width. Rommel was in a strong defensive position with no open flanks around which the enemy could maneuver, with defenses several miles deep, including 500,000 mines, strong artillery, and manned by tough and resolute troops. Mine clearance was difficult and dangerous. An electronic type of mine detector was perfected by two officers of the Polish Free Forces, and a limited number were available by late summer. The traditional method was probing carefully with a bayonet!

Ann Lane's article, "The Inevitable Victory? El Alamein Revisited," [278] Imperial War Museum *Review*, discusses Montgomery's impact on the ordinary soldier. Her research was based on the oral history (sound recording) collection of the Imperial War Museum. One soldier said that before Montgomery, "the only generals' names the troops knew were German names." Rommel had come to seem invincible, a "bogey-man."

A fascinating side of the El Alamein battle were the activities designed to mislead the Axis as to where the main point of attack would take place. Geoffrey Barkas, who directed the effort codenamed *Bartram*, wrote *The Camouflage Story: From Aintree to Alamein* [19]. It was the most elaborate deception scheme yet devised in North Africa. Hundreds of realistic-looking, dummy vehicles and guns were made as part of the effort. Was *Bartram* successful? In *Ultra and Mediterranean Strategy* [32], Ralph Bennett states that evidence is mixed: the Germans did not think the British attack would come as far south as deception planners hoped. However, the camouflage devices did deceive German reconnaisance pilots. Their reports, even just before British guns opened fire on October 23 were still, "Quiet day. No change." The 8th Army achieved complete tactical surprise.

Rommel's position before El Alamein is described in David Fraser's, *Knight's Cross: A Life of Field Marshal Erwin Rommel* [166]. Rommel's Panzer Army Africa consisted of ten divisions, four of which were German (the two armored were the 15th and 21st Panzer Divisions) the rest Italian. Of the Italian divisions, two were armored, the *Littorio* and *Ariete* Divisions. Total tank strength numbered about 500. To strengthen his line, Rommel "corseted" Italian units between German units so that no long section of the line was held by Italians alone. Rommel had 500 guns and 350 aircraft. On September 22, he returned to Germany for treatment of his stomach ailments; General Georg Stumme replaced Rommel. On October 24, Rommel received a telephone call from Hitler---bad news from Africa, "Do you feel well enough to go back?" He was not but left anyway, and arrived at the front on October 25 to find a battle raging at El Alamein.

At 9:40 pm, on October 23, 1942, some 500 British and Commonwealth guns opened fire on the enemy's batteries and illuminated the eastern sky. At 10 pm, four British divisions crossed the starting line. The battle of El Alamein had begun. Montgomery has received more praise than blame for his conduct of the battle. In his essay on Montgomery in *The Causes of Wars and Other Essays* [223], Michael Howard states that when his original plan did not work, Montgomery's real talent then showed when he switched his attack from one point to another. Instead of claiming credit for such tactical flexibility, Montgomery always insisted that everything had gone according to plan. He also displayed a willingness to sacrifice tanks (if not tank crews) rather than infantry.

On November 2, Hitler ordered Rommel to "hold on, do not yield a step...victory or death." Rommel carried out the order for 24 hours, then began the long 2,000-mile retreat with what was left of his Panzer Army.

In his 25th Anniversary narrative of the battle, which appeared in *Alamein and the Desert War* [245], Montgomery noted, "We could not have won the battle in twelve days without that magnificent 9th Australian Division." While the majority of "British" troops at El Alamein were from the Empire and Commonwealth, the heaviest losses were borne by United Kingdom forces (58 percent). The statistics are found in the official British history, *The Destruction of the Axis Forces in Africa* [382] by I.S.O. Playfair and C.J.C. Molony. The authors praised the German troops who had "put up a magnificent defence and retained their soldierly qualities in the face of stronger forces." Italian formations had fought with "spirit" but had been inadequately equipped and were "out-classed."

Military historian John Keegan, in his impressive study, *The Second World War* [255], declared that Montgomery's debut on the battlefield had been one of the most brilliant in the history of generalship.

For the British people, El Alamein marked the end of a succession of disasters and years of enduring bombs, bereavement, deprivation, discomfort, and lonely grandeur. There was at last something to celebrate, and Churchill ordered that church bells be rung from one end of Britain to the other for the first time in more than three years. Churchill wrote in the *The Hinge of Fate* [92]: "Before Alamein we never had a victory; After Alamein we never had a defeat." "Almost" is a necessary qualification, considering the earlier victories in Africa and some of the later setbacks in Europe. That being said, Churchill was correct when he wrote that "It marked in fact the turning of the 'Hinge of Fate.'"

The British film *Desert Victory* [131], produced by the 8th Army's Film unit, was Britain's answer to Stalin's film of the battle for Stalingrad. President Roosevelt considered *Desert Victory* "about the best thing that has been done about the war on either side."

Additional British and Commonwealth accounts include Anthony Farrar-Hockley, *The War in the Desert* [154]; B.L. Bernstein, *The Tide turned at Alamein: Impressions of the Desert War with the South African Division and the Eighth Army, June 1941-January 1943* [35]; Volume IV in the official British history series by I.S.O. Playfair and C.J.C. Molony, *The Destruction of the Axis Forces in Africa* [382]; the Australian official history by Barton Maughan, *Tobruk and El Alamein*

[321]; the Indian official history by P.C. Bharucha, *The North African Campaign, 1940-1943* [38]; the New Zealand official history by Ronald Walker, *Alam Halfa and Alamein* [481].

A classic memoir of the battle is that by the poet Keith Douglas, *Alamein to Zem Zem* [138]. An excerpt is included in *The Norton Book of Modern War* [172] edited by Paul Fussell. Douglas was later killed in Normandy. A terrifying vignette of the desert war by the New Zealander Dan Davin is included by Mordecai Richler in his work, *Writers on World War II: An Anthology* [399]. For sheer humor there is the memoir of Spike Milligan (formerly of the "Goon Show" with Peter Sellers), *"Rommel?"- "Gunner Who?": A Confrontation in the Desert* [333].

Two Italian accounts, both by participants, are Guilliano Palladino's *Peace at Alamein* and Paolo Caccia-Dominioni's, *Alamein 1933-1962: An Italian Story* [69]. Palladino, a junior office captured at El Alamein, wrote his very readable memoir in the form of a novel.

A German perspective on El Alamein was presented by General Fritz Bayerlein's essay in the 1956 book *Fatal Decisions* [167] edited by Seymour Freidin. According to Bayerlein, the inability to mount an amphibious assault on Malta contributed to the German defeat at El Alamein, which in his view was primarily a battle of supply. Blaming Hitler, Goering, or the enemy's material superiority for every defeat became a common feature of most post-war German military memoirs.

A much more accurate assessment is found in the official German history by Charles Burdick, *Unternehmen Sonnenblume* [66]; Other useful accounts are F.W. von Mellenthin's, *Panzer Battles* [478] and Wolf Heckmann's, *Rommel's War in Africa* [204].

THE DESERT AIR FORCE

The official British history of the Royal Air Force was written by D. Richards and H. Saunders, *Royal Air Force 1939-45*, volume II, *The Fight Avails* [397]. Referring to the contribution of the Desert Air Force, Montgomery said, "I punched him [Rommel] on the nose while Tedder bit his tail." Relations between Air Marshal Arthur Tedder and Montgomery eventually soured, and they grew to dislike each other intensely. Tedder's side of the story is found in his memoir *With Prejudice: The War Memoirs of Marshal of the Royal Air Force Lord Tedder* [459].

The wartime account (published in 1944), *Middle East, 1940-1942: A Study in Air Power* [194] by Philip Guedalla presented an idealized and distorted view of Army-Air cooperation. In their study, *Fire-Power: British Army Weapons and Theories of War 1904-1945* [39], Shelford Bidwell and Dominick Graham claimed that the "whole vexed problem of air support for the Army had been settled by the end of the Desert War in Africa." Alas, such was not the case. The attitude of the Air Marshals toward close ground support for the army is discussed in both John Terraine's *A Time for Courage: The Royal Air Force in the European War, 1939-1945* [461] and Vincent Orange's, *Coningham: A Biography of Air Marshal Sir*

Arthur Coningham [358]. Tedder was Coningham's influential patron and neither airman favored the use of aircraft at the front lines as supermobile artillery. American Air Chief Carl Spaatz described Coningham as a "combination of Bob Olds and Billy Mitchell, with possibly a bit of MacArthur thrown in for good measure." Coningham's dislike of Montgomery grew to the point where it was unequalled in bitterness by any of the better-known quarrels of the war.

Details concerning planes and pilots are found in *Fighters Over The Desert: The Air Battles in the Western Desert June 1940 to December 1942* [425] by Christopher Shores and Hans Ring. Both Axis and Commonwealth air forces are examined by the British and German authors. Before his death at the age of 22. German pilot Jochen Marseille claimed 158 victories to his credit. In German newspapers he was called "The African Eagle."

PURSUIT

Whatever criticisms have been aimed at Montgomery's generalship at El Alamein, they pale in comparison to the barrage of criticism leveled at him because of his failure to utterly destroy Rommel's army. In the official British history, *The Destruction of the Axis Forces in Africa* [382], authors I.S.O. Playfair and C.J.C. Molony comment that whether the 8th Army could have captured or destroyed more of Rommel's forces will be argued "as long as military history is read."

In an unforgettable analogy, in *The Desert Generals* [22] Correlli Barnett declared that Montgomery's pursuit of Rommel "showed all the bustling confidence of an archdeacon entering a brothel." In his highly critical assessment, *Brute Force: Allied Strategy and Tactics in the Second World War* [145], John Ellis commented that Montgomery "waddled tortoise-like behind Rommel across North Africa.

General Francis Tuker, the outspoken commander of the 4th Indian Division, and author of *Approach to Battle* [469], criticized what he called a "squandered" opportunity to annihilate Rommel's entire army. Even Ronald Lewin in his otherwise favorable biography, *Montgomery as Military Commander* [285], faulted him for allowing Rommel to escape. An O'Connor, Patton, or Rommel, declared Lewin, would have smashed what was left of the Panzerarmee. In an otherwise favorable treatment of Montgomery, General E.K.G. Sixsmith in his study, *British Generalship in the Twentieth Century* [428], regretted that "The pursuit was the most disappointing part of Montgomery's battle." On the other hand, the British had escaped from Rommel's grasp on earlier occasions.

In volume two of his magnificent biography, *Master of the Battlefield: Monty's War Years 1942-1944* [198], Nigel Hamilton largely attributed the "bungled" opportunities to cut off Rommel's retreat to the incompetence of certain tank commanders. Hamilton does think that Montgomery should have sent a stronger force across the desert to cut off the retreat at Benghazi. This missed opportunity is seen by Hamilton as the first evidence of excessive caution by Montgomery after El Alamein.

It is the *Ultra* disclosures since the 1970s, however, which have given renewed impetus to the charge that Montgomery missed a golden opportunity to destroy Rommel after El Alamein. F.H. Hinsley, the author of the official British history,

British Intelligence in the Second World War [215], expressed frustration over Montgomery's failure to attack Rommel when he was down to just 11 tanks immediately after El Alamein.

Historian Ralph Bennett, in his work *Ultra and Mediterranean Strategy* [32], declared that *Ultra* evidence "powerfully supports these criticisms" of missed opportunities to cut off Rommel's retreat before he reached Tunisia. Bennett is on less sure ground when he claims that the whole Allied strategy in the Mediterranean was "lastingly affected by what did not happen during November 1942." Had Rommel's forces been annihilated, Bennett believes the war in North Africa might have been shortened by six months. In the realm of "ifs" and "might-have-beens," Hitler might still have intervened in Tunisia to protect his southern flank, regardless of Rommel's fate.

Codebreakers: The Inside Story of Bletchley Park [214], edited by F.H. Hinsley and Alan Stripp, and published in 1993, is a collection of essays by those who worked at Bletchley Park during World War II. In Bennett's own essay, he mentions that he was on temporary service in Cairo and missed the "fierce indignation" in Hut 3 over Montgomery's slow pursuit of Rommel. Bennett found Montgomery's slowness "incomprehensible." A codebreaker who was present remembered well the frustration that exploded from Hut 3 at Montgomery's failure to overtake and destroy Rommel; he had not seen such an outburst among the codebreakers since the fighting six months earlier when Hut 3 believed it had provided enough intelligence to the 8th Army to avoid the "Cauldron" disaster.

In *The Causes of Wars and Other Essays* [223], Michael Howard remarked that the accusation that Montgomery had defeated Rommel, but had not destroyed him, was a legitimate criticism since Montgomery excelled in the set-piece battle and not pursuit. It would have been nice if Rommel could have been "put in the bag," declared Howard, but it would have changed the war only marginally.

Montgomery himself justified his actions in his *Memoirs* [337]. He insisted that he had not wanted to do anything silly and risk a setback after El Alamein. There were to be no more "Benghazi Handicap" which had seen previous British armies go back and forth across the desert.

And what of Rommel after El Alamein? In November, he wished "I were just a newspaper vendor in Berlin."

6

Torch: The Landings in French North Africa

At no time during the war did I experience a greater sense of relief than when, upon the following morning, I received a meager report to the effect that beach conditions were not too bad and the Casablanca landing was proceeding as planned. I said a prayer of thanksgiving; my greatest fear had been dissipated.

Eisenhower, *Crusade in Europe*

THE STRATEGIC DEBATE

A new phase of the war in North Africa opened on November 8, 1942, when American troops, together with British forces, landed in Morocco and Algeria, then French North Africa, as part of Operation *Torch*. The landings closed several months of transatlantic debate over Allied grand strategy. Since Pearl Harbor, the strategic question of the hour was what operations, if any, the United States and Britain should undertake in 1942. With the Soviet Union battling the bulk of the German army and Stalin demanding a Second Front, the two Western Allies could not wait until they were fully mobilized for action. At the Washington Conference in December 1941, Winston Churchill had proposed to President Franklin D. Roosevelt what was then called Operation *Gymnast*. What was later renamed *Torch*, called for the invasion of French North Africa by Allied forces which would then link up with the British 8th Army to the east and clear the whole of North Africa of the Axis.

General George C. Marshall, the U.S. Army Chief of Staff, strongly opposed the idea of a North African operation on the grounds that it would prevent a major cross-Channel assault in 1943. He favored a limited cross-Channel attack in 1942 (Operation *Sledgehammer*) to prepare the way for the main assault in 1943 (Operation *Roundup*). Marshall's own views can be found in *The Papers of George Catlett Marshall*. Vol. 3: *"The Right Man for the Job," December 7, 1941-May 31, 1943*, edited by Larry I. Bland and Sharon Ritenour Stevens, and published in 1991. The volume can be used as a reference source or read as a narrative account.

The four volume biography by Forrest C. Pogue, *George C. Marshall*, remains a fitting monument "to a giant among Anglo-American military leaders" (to quote the words of historian D. Clayton James). The strategic debate over what the new Anglo-American Allies should do in 1942 is covered in volume II of Pogue's work, *Ordeal and Hope, 1939-1942* [383].

The standard treatment of the American strategic tradition is Russell Weigley's, *The American Way of War: A History of United States Military Strategy and Policy*

[486]. Weigley views Marshall as the most able Allied strategist of World War II, and places him in the strategic tradition of Ulysses S. Grant. Whether Grantian or Clausewitzian, Marshall wanted to defeat Germany as quickly as possible so that the United States could turn all of its attention to Japan.

President Franklin D. Roosevelt decided in favor of *Torch*. On no other strategic decision of World War II did Marshall disagree so strongly with the President. Weigley has called the *Torch* decision "probably the most important Anglo-American strategic decision of the war."

Journalist and author, Norman Gelb in his 1992 book, *Desperate Venture: The Story of Operation Torch, the Allied Invasion of North Africa* [175], covers all the controversies of the campaign from its inception through the Axis surrender in May 1943. Gelb's basic conclusion is that the campaign was a mistake. Despite the benefits, Gelb believes that the cost of *Torch* was the delay of the decisive cross-Channel operation until 1944, as well as needless political turmoil and Anglo-French-American discord. Although his conclusion is neither new nor beyond serious questioning, Gelb's book is readable and worthwhile.

In his 1994 book, *Churchill and Roosevelt at War* [413], author Keith Sainsbury argued that on purely military grounds the two democratic leaders would have been wiser to have done nothing in 1942, and to have built up their strength for invading France in 1943. Yet, Sainsbury returns to the conclusion reached in his 1976 account, *North African Landings, 1942: A Strategic Decision* [414], that *Torch* was inevitable. Much more novel is the author's emphasis on Roosevelt's closer rapport with American naval thinking and his realization of the importance of the Mediterranean Sea to the Allied war effort. According to Sainsbury, it is more accurate to say that their strategic ideas coincided than to say Churchill persuaded Roosevelt to see things his way.

On the continuing historical controversy that *Torch* delayed the Second Front, Sainsbury contends that General Marshall's fear that *Torch* would prevent a cross-Channel operation became a self-fulfilling prophecy: willing to take great risks on *Sledgehammer*, Marshall was excessively cautious when it came to *Torch*. Two-thirds of the Anglo-American invasion force landed at the two western ports of Casablanca and Oran, hundreds of miles from Tunis. Sainsbury insists that it was Marshall's caution as much as the *Torch* decision which finally ruled out a cross-Channel assault in 1943. Churchill wanted Tunis by Christmas and a cross-Channel assault in 1943. He had to fight hard for an Allied landing even as far east as Algiers.

In his naval history, *Engage the Enemy More Closely: The Royal Navy in the Second World War* [21], Correlli Barnett argued forcefully that Winston Churchill's Mediterranean strategy tied up the British Empire's war effort for two years. He does not think the Mediterranean strategy, which led to the war in North Africa, was a rational or a "cost effective strategy" for the British.

Critics of *Torch* frequently point to the tremendous demands on Allied shipping required by the North African campaign. Those demands are brought out in *Merchant Shipping and the Demands of War* [30] by C.B.A. Behrens.

The tangled threads of decision making that led to *Torch* are traced in Richard W.

Steele's account, *The First Offensive, 1942: Roosevelt, Marshall and the Making of American Strategy*. Steele argues that given *Sledgehammer* (the proposal for a 1942 cross-Channel attack) was suicidal, and that Army Chief of Staff George C. Marshall was in a position to know the facts; in this instance, according to Steele, Roosevelt was "ill-served" by Marshall.

British Mediterranean/North African strategy is viewed in a favorable light by Michael Howard in his study, *The Mediterranean Strategy in the Second World War* [224]. According to Howard, clearing the North African shore of Axis forces and opening 'he Mediterranean to Allied shipping made good sense. Hardly foreseen at the time was the eventual capture of a quarter of a million Axis troops (including 100,000 Germans) in Tunisia, a larger haul than Stalingrad.

The unexpected benefits of the North African campaign are brought out by historian Gerhard Weinberg in his brilliant 1994 survey, *A World At Arms: A Global History of World War II* [487]. When *Torch* did not lead to the quick seizure of Tunis, and Hitler established a beachhead in Tunisia, the subsequent campaign drew massive Axis forces into a new theater of war at a time of crisis on the Eastern Front. Weinberg makes a convincing case that the North African campaign provided important relief to the Soviet Union, and made it impossible for the Germans to relieve Stalingrad: divisions could not be used in Tunisia and southern Russia at the same time, neither could German air transport be used in both places at once. Weinberg makes the crucial and frequently overlooked point that the two campaigns greatly assisted each other.

The decision to go to Africa was made on July 22, and Captain Harry C. Butcher noted in his diary that newly promoted Lieutenant-General Dwight D. Eisenhower thought the date "could well go down as the blackest day in history." Butcher, Eisenhower's naval aide, published the diary in 1946 as *My Three Years With Eisenhower: The Personal Diary of Captain Harry C. Butcher* [67]. Butcher's sometimes gossipy account is a valuable source concerning Eisenhower's wartime thoughts and actions.

In his biography, *Eisenhower* [5], historian Stephen E. Ambrose commented that Operation *Roundup*, which had been drawn up by Eisenhower when he was on the War Department Planning Staff, had the ring of Horace Greeley's "Forward to Richmond" cry in 1861. Only in the war three months, and with no combat-ready divisions, *Roundup* had called for coming to grips with the mighty Wehrmacht and Luftwaffe in 1943. Ambrose remarks half jokingly that considering how many mistakes Eisenhower made in the North African campaign, that alone is perhaps sufficient justification for *Torch* instead of *Roundup*.

In August, Eisenhower was appointed to lead what Ambrose calls "the first joint Anglo-American offensive since the French and Indian War." In that first Allied offensive against the Axis, Eisenhower would be hesitant, unsure of himself, and often depressed and irritable. Nineteen months later, declares Ambrose, Eisenhower and everyone else had improved dramatically---the payoff for *Torch* would be the stunning success of *Overlord* in 1944.

War correspondent Alan Moorehead in his *African Trilogy* [339] describes the scene in America shortly before the North African landings. His wartime observations lend powerful support to President Roosevelt's political instinct that American military action against the Axis in 1942 was absolutely vital. Recently arrived in America from the desert war, Moorehead sensed the public's discontent at the way the war was going, "Why don't they DO something? What's wrong with them? Why can't they start a second front?" On the morning of November 8, all the answers came suddenly together, wrote Moorehead: "I was in New York when the news broke, and the effect on the people was electric. They snatched at newspapers and they hung around their radio sets. They were aglow with the news. America was in it at last. At last we had a second front. At last we were hitting back."

If a 1942 cross-Channel assault was suicidal---the Dieppe Raid in August tended to prove that such was the case---and a do-nothing policy was politically out of the question, the Mediterranean operation in French North African was logical and compelling. The American and British people (not to mention Stalin) wanted Allied action, and so did the troops.

U.S. War Department plannning in 1942 is covered by Maurice Matloff and Edward M. Snell in their volume *Strategic Planning for Coalition Warfare*, volume one, *1941-1942* [319]; other volumes in the famous U.S. Army "Green Book" series include Richard M. Leighton and Robert W. Coakley, *Global Logistics and Strategy, 1940-1943* [282]; and Kent R. Greenfield, *Command Decisions* [190]; Ray S. Cline, *Washington Command Post: The Operations Division* [99]. Cline remarks that *Torch* was "hastily launched"; a sub-heading is titled, "Case History in Confusion."

A landmark in the literature of World War II are the volumes edited by Alfred D. Chandler, Jr., and Stephen E. Ambrose, *The Papers of Dwight David Eisenhower: The War Years*, volume II [87]. They are an invaluable source of information on Eisenhower and the isssues that confronted him as Allied Supreme Commander; Equally indispensable to the researcher, and fascinating for the general reader, is Warren F. Kimball's, *Churchill and Roosevelt: The Complete Correspondence* [262]; the views of the U.S. Chiefs of Staff are found in Ernest J. King and Walter M. Whitehill, *Fleet Admiral King: A Naval Record* [263], and H.H. Arnold, *Global Mission* [9]. Also at the center of decision making was William Leahy, *I Was There: The Personal Story of the Chief of Staff to Presidents Roosevelt and Truman* [281].

Official British accounts of the planning for *Torch* include J.R.M. Butler, *Grand Strategy* [68] and Michael Howard, *Grand Strategy* [222]. Besides Churchill's own epic five volume history, *The Second World War* [90], biographer Martin Gilbert's monumental, multivolume *Winston S. Churchill* [177] offers almost day by day coverage of Churchill's wartime decisions.

OPERATION *TORCH*

Eisenhower's own feelings of anxiety before his first D-Day experience are found in *The Papers of Dwight David Eisenhower* [87] edited by Alfred D. Chandler, Jr., and Stephen E. Ambrose. *Torch* was the largest and most complicated combined operation in history to that date. In the judgment of Eisenhower, it was an undertaking "of a quite desperate nature." Would the Vichy French authorities in North Africa cooperate, as hoped, or would they fight? Would Spain's fascist leader Franco choose this critical moment to enter the war on Hitler's side?

Not until September 5 did the Allies decide exactly where they were to land. Churchill had to insist on Algiers and even this was 500 miles away from Tunis, the "milk of the whole coconut," in Eisenhower's apt description. The date set for *Torch* was November 8, only two months after the final decision to land at Casablanca, Oran, and Algiers, and not much time to plan and organize the deployment of three task forces comprising more than 70,000 troops, more than 400 warships, and upward of 60 merchant ships. The Western Task Force, consisting of the 2nd Armored, 3rd and 9th Divisions, sailed directly from the United States; Central Task Force, comprising the U.S. 1st Armored Division and part of the future 82nd Airborne Division, sailed from Britain; Eastern Task Force, composed of the British 78th and U.S. 34th Divisions, also sailed from the United Kingdom.

The Period of Balance [407], volume two in the official British naval history, *The War at Sea 1939-1945* by Stephen Roskill, describes the naval side of *Torch*. Another essential naval source is *A Sailor's Odyssey* [121], the personal narrative of Admiral Andrew B. Cunningham, the Commander-in-Chief of the British Fleet in the Mediterranean. The straightforward and modest Cunningham became one of Eisenhower's closest British friends. Fresh and stimulating insights into the Mediterranean naval campaign are offered by Correlli Barnett in his book, *Engage the Enemy More Closely: The Royal Navy in the Second World War* [21].

American Admiral H. Kent Hewitt commanded the Western Naval Task Force that carried General George C. Patton, Jr., and his 35,000 troops to capture Casablanca and Port Lyautey on the coast of French Morocco. American naval operations involved in *Torch* are covered in volume two, *Operations in North African Waters October 1942-June 1943* [344], of Samuel Eliot Morison's majesterial series, *History of United States Naval Operations in World War II*. Hewitt later wrote the article, "The Landings in Morocco, November 1942," for the *United States Naval Institute Proceedings* [207]. In her study, *Viking of Assault: Admiral John Leslie Hall, Jr., and Amphibious Warfare* [182], Susan H. Godson focused on Hewitt's chief of staff. Hall oversaw naval planning and training in Norfolk, Virginia. Neither sailors nor soldiers had time for sufficient training. The rehearsals for *Torch* that were held in Chesapeake Bay did not go smoothly. An ice cream vendor waited on the supposedly secret beach to refresh the troops when they landed! General Patton was prompted to say "Never in history has the Navy landed an army at the planned time and place. If you land us anywhere within fifty miles of Fedala and within one week of D-Day, I'll go ahead and win."

Patton's own memoir, *War As I Knew It* [369], was taken from the plain-speaking diary which he personally kept until four days before his fatal automobile accident. Hastily written, his narrative was blunt and peppery. The bulk of the book concerns the 3rd Army's campaign in Europe and there is no discussion of the Tunisian campaign except for a description of the Victory Parade held in Tunis on May 20,

1943. Probably the best American field commander since Stonewall Jackson, Patton was indispensable in a shooting war.

On arrival, French ships gave the American task force a hard fight. When the French ships moved to attack the transports, the *Augusta* and other vessels beat them off. On November 9, the unfinished French battleship *Jean Bart* fired its 15-inch guns at the *Augusta*, which wisely moved out of range. In Oran the resistance was heavy, and at Algiers two British destroyer was sunk attempting to force an entrance in the harbor against Vichy opposition. No French soldier had paid the slighest attention to General Henri Giraud, the anti-Vichy general whom the Allies had brought to North Africa for the purpose of rallying his countrymen to the Allied cause. On November 10, Vichy Admiral Jean Darlan finally ordered a cease-fire.

Writer of popular military history, William B. Breuer authored the 1986 account, *Operation Torch: The Allied Gamble to Invade North Africa* [59]. Highly suitable for general readership, the book is a compelling, journalistic narrative of the Allied invasion that offers a wealth of detail; Other sources on *Torch* include Blumenson's, *The Patton Papters: 1940-1945* [48]; Edward Ellsberg, *No Banners, No Bugles* [146]; Monroe MacCloskey, *Torch and the Twelth Air Force* [303]; Brahim Harouni's doctoral dissertation, "How the Anglo-American Invasion of North Africa in November 1942 was Prepared and Realised," [203]; and Jack Coggins's, *The Campaign for North Africa* [103], which contains maps, diagrams, and drawings of the weapons and equipment used by both sides in Africa. The story of American correspondents present at the *Torch* landings is found in M.L. Stein's work, *Under Fire: The Story of American War Correspondents* [442].

THE DARLAN AFFAIR

Hopes for *Torch* were only partly realized. The Allies had anticipated that the French in North Africa would quickly turn from Vichy and join the Allied effort against the Axis. Roosevelt's optimism is revealed in *Churchill and Roosevelt: The Complete Correspondence* [262] edited by Warren F. Kimball. The President wrote to Churchill in September: "An American expedition led in all three phases by American officers will meet little resistance from the French Army in Africa."

The American Consul General in Algiers, Robert Murphy, played a key role in America's first offensive in World War II. An indispensable personal account, Murphy's memoir, *A Diplomat Among Warriors* [347], is candid and entertaining. In London before the landings, he assured Eisenhower and his officers that French North Africa was more like California than a tropical wilderness. He advised before *Torch* that it must appear to be an American operation and must not include any of General Charles de Gaulle's Free French forces. The Vichy French in North Africa were hostile toward de Gaulle and the British.

A different perspective is found in Harold MacMillan's autobiography, *The Blast of War, 1939-1945* [311]. MacMillan (future Prime Minister) was appointed by Churchill to serve as British political representative on Eisenhower's staff in Algiers. He provides perceptive descriptions of persons and events involved in the French

North African political scene. In *The Blast of War*, MacMillan looked at each problem in an orderly fashion. In his 1984 book, *War Diaries: Politics and War in the Mediterranean, January 1943- May 1945*, the reader sees several crises going on at the same time. The *War Diaries* were MacMillan's daily entries into his diary, He remarked that Robert Murphy had "the American anti-de Gaulle complex."

Cloak-and-dagger operations in French North Africa are described in one of the more honest, forceful, and colorful military memoirs of World War II, *Calculated Risk* [94] by General Mark Clark. Landed at night from a British submarine at Cherchel, 90 miles from Algiers, on October 21, 1942, Clark was to contact local anti-Petainists (Philippe Petain was the leader of Vichy France) in preparation for the Allied landing. Clark had a close escape when French police raided the house where the anti-Vichy group were meeting. In the confused scene that followed, the American general lost his pants when the kayak he was paddling out to the waiting submarine capsized in the waves.

In the 1960s, while serving as President of The Citadel, The Military College of South Carolina, Mark Clark was instrumental in obtaining the periscope from the submarine through which he first glimpsed the North African shoreline. The HMS *Seraph* monument is located on the campus of the The Citadel, in Charleston, commemorating the first combined Allied operation in World War II. Lieutenant Norman Jewell, commander of the submarine, wrote *Secret Submarine Mission* [246].

The Vichy response to the Allied landings in North Africa is discussed by Gerhard Weinberg in *A World At Arms: A Global History of World War II* [487]. Weinberg is scathingly critical of the Vichy French forces in North Africa. The French military authorities there remained obedient to Marshal Pétain and offered no resistance to the arrival of Axis forces when Hitler decided to fight for Tunisia. In contrast, the Vichy French fired on the Allied troops who landed to the west, inflicting considerable casualties. Weinberg remarks bitterly that Pétain had performed his last major service for the Germans: there would be a major campaign for Tunisia and hence no Allied landing in the West in 1943. That in turn meant France could look forward to an additional year of German occupation.

The Allies had hoped to install General Henri Giraud, an escaped POW, as head of French forces in North Africa, but they quickly discovered he had no influence with anyone when the Vichy French opened fire at the beaches and landing sites. By an extraordinary coincidence, Admiral Jean Darlan, Petain's commander-in-chief, happended to be in Algiers to see his son who was stricken with polio. For two years, Darlan had been broadcasting anti-British and anti-De Gaulle statements from Vichy, and apparently collaborating closely with the Germans. For his own opportunistic reasons, Darlan ordered French commanders to cease fighting against the Allies. When Eisenhower signed an agreement with the former Vichy leader, much of the Allied press and public exploded in rage. The Allies appeared to be adopting a policy of expediency rather than following the idealism of the Atlantic Charter.

Robert O. Paxton's *Vichy France: Old Guard and New Order, 1940-1944* [370], is the standard work on the subject. The preeminent authority on Vichy France, Paxton is highly critical of both the Vichy regime and Darlan, whom Paxton views as one of the principal architects of collaboration with Nazi Germany. Darlan once told Roosevelt's emissary, Admiral Leahy, "come with a large army we will join you; if you come with a small one we will fight you."

Darlan was assassinated on Christmas eve 1942. General Mark Clark regarded his death "as a gift from heaven." He had served his purpose in allowing the quick occupation of Morocco and Algeria without a heavy loss of Allied lives. The controversial Darlan is the subject of a French biography by Hervé Coutau-Begarie and Claude Huan, *Darlan* [114].

Anthony Verrier's, *Assassination in Algiers: Churchill, Roosevelt, de Gaulle, and the Murder of Admiral Darlan* [477] is based largely on innuendos and dubious interpretations. An objective treatment of the French political scene in North Africa is the study, *The Politics of Torch: The Allied Landings and the Algiers Putsch, 1942* [171], by Arthur Layton Funk.

The Free French cause is magnificently presented by its leader Charles de Gaulle in his autobiography, *The War Memoirs of Charles de Gaulle* [130]. The Darlan deal understandably enraged de Gaulle. De Gaulle was not informed in advance about the Allied expedition to North Africa because of the concern over security.

In his book, *Crusade in Europe* [143], Eisenhower defended his agreement with Darlan. He commented that French sentiment in North Africa did not "remotely" agree with what they had been led to expect. They had been led to believe that a French population, bitterly resentful of Vichy-Nazi domination, would greet the Allies as deliverers. Instead, Eisenhower heard, "Why did you bring this war to us? We were satisfied before you came to get us all killed."

At least Eisenhower could take comfort in the fact that Morocco and Algeria were now in Allied hands. To the east, in Tunisia, it was different. Already, German units had reached Tunis by air. From November 9 onward they reinforced as rapidly as possible.

7

The Tunisian Campaign

American soldiers who survived the bitter months of January and February 1943 in Tunisia will never forget them---or forget Tunisia. For it was during this period in the deserts and mountains that American forces first crossed swords with veteran German legions and learned war from them in the hard way. These American soldiers, suffering from faults in leadership, from their own ignorance, from inferior equipment, reeled in defeat and yet rose to victory.

General Lucian K. Truscott, *Command Missions*

TUNIS BY CHRISTMAS

After successfully landing in French Morocco and Algeria, the main Allied objective was Tunis, the capital and chief port of Tunisia. If Tunis, together with Bizerta, could be captured quickly, what was left of Rommel's defeated Axis army would be destroyed between General Eisenhower's Allied forces moving eastward and Montgomery's 8th Army, then 1,200 miles away, moving westward. The task of seizing Tunis was entrusted to General Kenneth Anderson's First British Army, which in practice consisted of only a small inexperienced force.

Fearful of a possible German attack through Spain, two thirds of the Allied assault forces had landed at Casablanca and Oran, and were thus too far way to support a quick advance on Tunis. As a result the force that set out from Algiers to seize Tunis, 560 miles away, was too weak for such an important mission.

Speed and boldness on the part of Anderson might have resulted in the capture of Tunis, but the day after the Allies began their landings in northwest Africa Hitler began pouring troops into Tunisia. Another complication was the undetermined attitude of the local French forces.

The Axis buildup was much quicker and more powerful than predicted; Hitler had decided at once. He was not going to give up Tunisia without a fight. In his book *Hitler's Mistakes* [283], Ronald Lewin called the decision "a grave miscalculation" on Hitler's part to pour men and supplies into the "Tunisian deathtrap" when the critical Russian front needed additional strength. Unlike Hitler (and Kesselring), Rommel favored a quick withdrawal to the line of the Alps---to the frontier of a Fortress Germany. Biographer David Fraser treats Rommel's strategic views sympathetically in *Knight's Cross: A Life of Field Marshal Erwin Rommel* [166]. If Plan Orient was dead, what were they all doing in North Africa, asked Rommel? Such thinking was regarded as defeatist and unduly pessimistic.

The Allied advance stopped 15 miles from Tunis on November 28. By that time, the Germans had flown in 15,000 combat infantry, with supporting armor, while

Anderson led only a few thousand men in a reconnaissance in force. Eisenhower's account of what had gone wrong can be found in *Crusade in Europe* [143] and in *The Papers of Dwight David Eisenhower: The War Years: II* [87]. His private frustrations and irritations, as opposed to his public good cheer and optimism which was of enormous value for morale, were recorded by Butcher in his diary, *My Three Years with Eisenhower* [67]. Not to be overlooked are many of Eisenhower's personal letters, which are to be found in *Letters to Mamie* [142] edited by his son, John S.D. Eisenhower.

In his study *Eisenhower* [5], Stephen E. Ambrose sharply disagreed with Eisenhower's portrayal of himself in *Crusade in Europe* as one who took chances, as having taken a "great gamble" in rushing Anderson to Tunis. In the opinion of Ambrose, after being a staff officer for 20 years Eisenhower was too orderly and cautious too. Instead of going to the front to galvanize Anderson, Eisenhower stayed in Algiers and devoted his time to politics and securing his rear areas. Ambrose wonders what a Patton or Rommel might have accomplished in such circumstances. Perhaps, but the Germans remained extremely dangerous.

A good summary of the reasons for the Allied failure to reach Tunis is in the official U.S. Army Air Forces history, *Europe: Torch to Pointblank* [117], by Wesley Frank Craven and James Lea Cate. General Kenneth Anderson gave enemy air action as a major reason, especially the persistent Stuka dive-bombing of his forward troops. Allied P-38s and Spitfires were outnumbered by Me-109s and FW-190s. The closest Allied airfield to the front line was a hundred miles away, and the enemy's were within 15 miles.

Anderson's First Army was 400 miles from Algiers, and linked by extremely poor roads. The Axis forces, on the other hand, had to make only a short crossing from Sicily (100 miles), and could then quickly distribute supplies and reinforcements. Designated the Fifth Panzer Army, the main Axis formations sent over to Tunisia were the 10th Panzer Division, part of the Hermann Goering Panzer Division, the 334 Infantry Division, and the Italian Superga Division. General Jurgen von Arnim assumed command on December 9, taking over from General Walther Nehring who had previously directed the Axis defense of Tunis.

The Tunisian campaign is described in detail by Gregory Blaxland in his book, *The Plain Cook and the Great Showman: The First and Eighth Armies in North Africa* [44]. The author served with the First Army in Tunisia and he attempts to rectify the "deep rooted neglect" of First Army and its commander whom Montgomery called a "plain cook" (later, his opinion dropped even lower and Anderson became a bad chef). The "Great Showman" in the title refers to Montgomery. First Army casualties were over 25,000 in the Tunisian campaign (slightly over four thousand killed), compared to the 8th Army's 12,000 casualties (2,139 killed). Blaxland remarks that only the loan of mules from the French, which brought them their food and a daily ration of rum, made possible the troops survival in the mud of the Tunisian hills, which had been soaked by drenching December rains. The British quickly formed their own mule trains.

Perceptive observations and criticisms of the Allied campaign in Tunisia can be found in Philip Jordan's book, *Jordan's Tunis Diary* [249]. The war correspondent wrote that "Without any question we have run up against a great deal more than we anticipated, and we haven't got enough air support." Jordan criticized continued attacks when it was clear they had "walked into a stone wall."

A brief personnal narrative of the early days in Tunisia was provided by American film director Darryl F. Zanuck in his short account, *Tunis Expedition* [502]. A reviewer noted that Zanuck was no Hollywood glamor boy satisfied with sitting on the sidelines. A colonel in the signal corps, Zanuck moved from Claridge's Hotel in London to cowering in a slit trench in Tunisia as he made the documentary film *At the Front*. With the atrocious winter weather turning all roads into quagmires, a disappointed Eisenhower called a halt to Tunisian operations on Christmas Eve 1942. In the words of Craven and Cate, "*Torch* had failed of complete success." Charles Messenger's, *The Tunisian Campaign* [330] is a well-illustrated, well-told story, but it is not new.

THE BATTLE OF KASSERINE PASS (FEBRUARY 14-23, 1943)

The Germans and Italians fielded a considerable force in Tunisia, amounting to over 11 divisions. However, their supply situation became critical; "Sink, burn and destroy. Let nothing pass." That was Admiral Andrew Cunningham's signal to ships on patrol in the Sicilian Channel in May 1943. The naval effort against Axis convoys is described in his memoir, *A Sailor's Odyssey* [121]. The Axis airlift suffered similar heavy losses from Allied air power.

The best overall account of American military operations in Tunisia is the official U.S. Army "Green Book" volume, *Northwest Africa: Seizing the Initiative in the West* [226] by George F. Howe. The Allied line extended over a vast front of more than 250 miles. It stretched all the way from the Mediterranean on the north to the bleak edge of the Sahara desert on the south. In the north the British First Army clung to its positions in the mountains that rimmed Bizerta and Tunis. In the center a ragged assortment of French battalions under General Alphonse Juin held 100 miles of the front. To the south, guarding the right flank of the Allied line was the U.S. II Corps commanded by General Lloyd Fredendall.

Stephen E. Ambrose covers the Tunisian campaign in *The Supreme Commander: The War Years of General Dwight D. Eisenhower* [6], volume one of his masterful two-volume biography of the Allied Supreme Commander and later President of the United States. Eisenhower worried most about the area held by the U.S. II Corps, which was composed of the 1st Armored Division, the 1st Infantry Division, and the 34th Division, with the 9th Infantry Division in reserve. None of these divisions had had any combat experience except for the brief fight with the Vichy French back in November. They had all been sent to North Africa before they had time for thorough training in the United States. According to Ambrose, they were "complacent, poorly disciplined, unprepared for what they would shortly have to face."

On the other side of the hill, Axis forces were preparing to attack. Rommel, instead of finding himself caught between the pincers of Eisenhower's forces and those of Montgomery, had retired to join General Jurgen von Arnim's Fifth Panzer Army which could now strike at either or both its enemies from a strong central position. Von Arnim and Rommel decided in early February that the enemy's situation in southern Tunisia was ripe for a counter-stroke.

What happened next is skillfully described by Martin Blumenson in his account, *Kasserine Pass* [45], the first major engagement of World War II in which the American Army fought directly against the seasoned, battle-experienced veterans of the German Wehrmacht. In a series of engagements collectively known as the Battle of Kasserine Pass, the U.S. II Corps of 30,000 men suffered over 3,000 casualties, including 300 killed, and an additional 3,000 missing in action. II Corps had lost 183 tanks. Kasserine destroyed the overconfidence that had been growing in the American forces since the *Torch* landings and led to some much needed reforms, and at the same time it helped awaken the American public to the hard reality that victory over the Axis was still a long way off. Blumenson, who was a senior U.S. Army civilian historian, explored the factors leading to defeat, among the most important being the lack of combat experience.

General Lucian K.Truscott, Jr., provides an excellent behind-the-scenes look at the Allied command structure before Kasserine in his outstanding World War II memoir, *Command Missions: A Personal Story* [468]. Truscott commented that not all their troubles in Tunisia were of German, or even French origin; "Personality Problems" loom large in explaining the Kasserine debacle. In particular there was the problem with General Lloyd Fredendall, II Corps commander. Small in stature, loud and rough in speech, he was critical of superiors and subordinates alike. Fredendall was excessively concerned with the safety of his command post which he located some 65 miles behind the front lines in an enormous underground bunker that two hundred combat engineers had labored for weeks to construct. He rarely left it. Truscott remarked that most American officers who saw this command post were embarrassed, and their comments were usually caustic. In his book *World War II in the Mediterranean 1942-1945* [126], military historian Carlo D'Este calls Fredendall "a shockingly inept commander."

The German attack jumped off at daylight on St.Valentine's Day, February 14, 1943. The divisional history by George F. Howe, *The Battle History of the 1st Armored Division: "Old Ironsides"* [227] describes what happened to elements of the 1st Armored Division: more than 200 German tanks, supported overhead by Stuka dive-bombers, stormed through Faid Pass and the small village of Sidi Bou Zid. Near Sbeitla, an American armored counterattack was detroyed; in two days, more than 100 American tanks had been knocked-out. Eventually, remarks Howe, the bitter truth was accepted, "The Division had been walloped."

The Axis attack swept on through the narrow three-mile gap, known as Kasserine Pass and threatened the Allied base at Tebessa. The 34th Infantry Division, a former National Guard unit, lost the better part of a regiment made up of many soldiers from Iowa. Not until the evening of February 21 was the panzer attack halted by tanks of the British 6th Armored Division rushed south for reinforcement, and American artillery of the 9th Infantry Division which had raced day and night 750 miles from

Oran over ice-sheeted mountain roads. Early on the morning of February 23 the Germans withdrew through Kasserine Pass after winning what General Omar Bradley called a "significant victory."

An essential source for American operations in Tunisia is General Ernest N. Harmon's personal narrative, *Combat Commander: Autobiography of a Soldier* [202]. His memoir is a frank and critical assessment of people and events. Despatched by Eisenhower to help restore order in the II Corps sector, Harmon went to see General Fredendall when the Battle of Kasserine Pass was over; he found the corps commander in bed, showing the effects of several drinks of whiskey he had taken to celebrate the Axis withdrawal. Harmon later reported to Eisenhower in Algiers: "Well," Eisenhower asked, "What do you think of Fredendall?" "He's no damned good. You ought to get rid of him," replied the gruff, no-nonsense Harmon who would become one of America's best World War II divisional commanders.

Eisenhower's role in this, his first real battle has been severely criticized. In the one-volume condensation of his earlier study, *Eisenhower: Soldier and President* [5], Stephen E. Ambrose called his performance "miserable." Eisenhower had been unwilling for too long to remove Fredendall, a protégé of General George C. Marshall. Eisenhower finally dismissed Fredendall and replaced him with General George S. Patton, Jr. Ambrose's exciting prose is underscored by his conviction that Eisenhower was "a great and good man."

In his memoir, *Crusade in Europe* [143], Eisenhower blamed his Intelligence officer (British Brigadier Eric E. Mockler-Ferryman) for relying too heavily on one source of intelligence information (*Ultra*) before Kasserine. Mockler-Ferryman had insisted that Intelligence indicated Rommel would attack in the north at Fondouk; in fact, the German high command had wanted just such an attack---that was the *Ultra* intercept Mockler-Ferryman acted on---but instead of following orders, Rommel had launched his own attack. Mockler-Ferryman was dismissed immediately after Kasserine.

Belonging to the sensationalized, potboiler genre is Charles Whiting's account, *Kasserine: The Battlefield Slaughter of American Troops by Rommel's Afrika Korps* [492]. The dean of popular "battle story" writers, Whiting relies heavily on Blumenson's work for his battle descriptions and Kay Summersby for other revealing tidbits.

PATTON

With sirens shrieking the arrival of General George S. Patton, Jr., a procession of armored vehicles wheeled into the dingy square opposite the schoolhouse that served as II Corps headquarters. Like a charioteer, Patton stood in the lead car, with his face scowling into the wind and his jaw strained against the web strap of a two-starred steel helmet. The above description is taken from Omar Bradley's memoir, *A Soldier's Story* [54], that indispensable account by one of the great American commanders of the war.

Bradley would succeed Patton as II Corps commander when Patton left to prepare for the invasion of Sicily. Although Bradley is sometimes critical of Patton in his memoir, the comments are far more biting in the second version, *A General's Life: An Autobiography* [55], which he wrote in collaboration with Clay Blair. Bradley died in 1981 before the book was completed, and Blair has described the result as "half Bradley, half Blair." In his later years, judging from *A General's Life*, Bradley was a cantankerous commentator on his wartime colleagues. Bradley served as a technical advisor to the 1970 film *Patton*.

The complexity and gusto of Patton can be found in *The Patton Papers 1885-1940* [48] edited by Martin Blumenson. The renowned military historian weaves a narrative around extracts from Patton's diaries, journals, letters, and speeches.

Blumenson authored a short, popular biography of this warrior-hero in 1986, *Patton: The Man Behind the Legend 1885-1945* [47].

An earlier biography was that by Ladislas Farago, *Patton: Ordeal and Triumph* [153]. Both fascinated and repelled by his hero, Farago endorses Patton's strategic ideas; the villains of the story are Montgomery, Eisenhower, and to a lesser degree, Bradley.

In his introduction to Patton's memoirs, *War As I Knew It* [369], Douglas Southall Freeman, the biographer of Robert E. Lee, hoped that Patton would find a competent biographer and that others would leave him alone. Most assuredly, Freeman would be delighted that military historian Carlo D'Este decided to write the first complete account of Patton's life. D'Este's 1995 biography, *Patton: A Genius For War* [124] addresses Patton's strengths and weaknesses in a scrupulously objective fashion. The author provides a fascinating portrait of the complex man behind the popular image. Suffering from dyslexia, Patton had a rage to excel. D'Este's book is based on primary sources and contains a 35-page bibliography.

Patton did for the U.S. II Corps what Montgomery had done earlier for the British 8th Army. Neither one of these commanders would tolerate amateurism. The easy-going days were over as Patton brought a new spirit to II Corps. Under Patton, in less than two weeks, II Corps went from defeat to success at the Battle of El Guettar. Patton told his staff the night before the attack: "Gentlemen, tomorrow we attack. If we are not victorious, let no one come back alive."

An armored battle group of the 10th Panzer Division was ambushed on the open plain by the 1st Infantry Division disposed in the hills overlooking the highway. An account of the Big Red One's actions in Tunisia is found in H.R. Knickerbocker's history of the famed division, *Danger Forward: The Story of the First Division in World War II* [270]. No divisional history ever suffered from over-modesty, but the praise is well-deserved in this case. During World War II, 43,743 men fought in the 1st Division.

Although El Guettar was a minor engagement by World War II standards, it showed that the U.S. Army was no longer an adversary to be taken lightly. General Ernest Harmon's account, *Combat Commander: Autobiography of a Soldier* [202], described the new era under Patton. Harmon was appointed to command the 1st Armored Division.

ALLIED UNITY

The importance of personal relations to the success of the Anglo-American partnership is emphasized in John S.D. Eisenhower's (Eisenhower's son), *Allies: Pearl Harbor to D- Day* [144]. Inter-Allied and interservice friction came to the surface when Patton complained bitterly about the air situation for what he called a "Total lack of air cover his forces." Air Vice-Marshal Arthur "Mary" Coningham, commander of the Allied North-West African Tactical Air Force, resented Patton's criticism and responded in a widely distributed signal that suggested American troops were not battleworthy. An outraged Patton demanded and got an apology from Coningham who was rebuked by Air Marshal Arthur Tedder. Eisenhower in turn upbraided Patton, reminding him of the necessity for Allied teamwork. An angry Patton felt Eisenhower had "sold out" to the British" and "Ike must go." Historian Stephen E. Ambrose, in his magnificent work, *The Supreme Commander: The War Years of General Dwight D. Eisenhower* [6] points out that Eisenhower was, in his own words, a fanatic on the subject of Allied unity. Nothing could be datelined "General Eisenhower's Headquarters." He insisted on the term "Allied Headquarters." Initially, recalled Eisenhower, the British and Americans came together like a bulldog and a cat. In *A Soldier's Story* [54], Omar Bradley remarked that as Supreme Commander in the Mediterranean Eisenhower walked a chalk line to avoid being branded pro-American by the British and pro-British by some American commanders. Bradley related that at the outset of the North African war there were some British officers who regarded the American Army with "ill-concealed amusement." In *Command Missions: A Personal Story* [468], Lucian K. Truscott, Jr. noted that American and British soldiers always got on well together whenever they came in contact. He claimed that the troubles occurred at higher levels---among the commanders and staff officers.

In Tunisia, Eisenhower had shown both strengths and weaknesses. His greatest success was welding an Allied team together, especially at AFHQ (Allied Forces Headquarters). He got along with others and he saw to it that British and American officers got along with each other.

THE ARMY-AIR CONTROVERSY

The Patton-Coningham spat not only reflected sensitive national feelings, but indicated the differences between the army commanders and their air force counterparts. Coningham's views are presented by his Vincent Orange in *Coningham: A Biography of Air Marshal Sir Arthur Coningham* [358]. Coningham believed less in close air support for ground forces than he did in strategic air strikes on the enemy's supply bases and gaining air superiority.

The U.S. official history, *Northwest Africa: Seizing the Initiative in the West* [226], by George F. Howe acknowledged that the Tunisian experience left the air and ground commanders in disagreement concerning the proper relationship of air and ground units. In his memoir, *Calculated Risk* [94], General Mark Clark noted the wide differences that existed between the airmen and the ground force commanders like himself who wanted specific air units placed under their command to serve as "flying artillery." Clark wrote, "It was a question that plagued us on many occasions throughout the war, and one that still does." While improvements were made in air-ground cooperation, the problem of providing close or direct ground support to soldiers on the battlefield was not solved in North Africa.

The British air point of view was expressed by Arthur Tedder in his memoir *With Prejudice: The War Memoirs of Marshal of the Royal Air Force Lord Tedder* [459]. British air thinking ran more to strategic missions than to close support of the ground forces. British doctrine is discussed by W.A. Jacobs in his article, "Air Support for the British Army, 1939-1943," *Military Affairs* [239]. British air doctrine grew among American air officers even though the American Air Force was still an integral part of the U.S. Army. American ground support doctrine is discussed in David Syrett's essay, "The Tunisian Campaign, 1942-43," in Benjamin F. Cooling's volume, *Case Studies in the Development of Close Air Support* [109]; Other treatments include Richard P. Hallion's, *Strike from the Sky: The History of Battlefield Air Attack 1911-1945* [196]; Daniel R. Mortensen's, *A Pattern for Joint Operations: World War II Close Air Support, North Africa* [345], and a personnal narrative by General Laurence S. Kuter, "Goddamnit, Georgie!" *Air Force Magazine* [276].

THE 8TH ARMY IN TUNISIA

Taking Tripoli on January 23 1943, Montgomery's 8th Army had moved inexorably along the North African coast. In the official U.S. history, *Northwest Africa: Seizing the Initiative in the West* [226], George F. Howe wrote that 8th Army had proceeded westward from Egypt with "the majestic deliberation of a pachyderm." The Tunisian campaign is covered in *The Destruction of the Axis Forces in Africa* [382], volume IV in the official British history series *The Mediterranean and Middle East* by I.S.O. Playfair and C.J.C. Molony. Eisenhower, Anderson, and Alexander (he possessed "strategic genius") are treated favorably, Montgomery considerably less so.

In his *Master of the Battlefield: Monty's War Years 1942-1944* [198], Nigel Hamilton asserts that whereas Eisenhower's Tunisian campaign "faltered and ground to a halt through over-dispersion, lack of energetic command, disastrously poor air force support, and fundamental lack of tactical expertise," Montgomery had conducted a "model campaign" in Tripolitania, refusing to play Rommel's game of opportunistic exploitation.

The Afrika Korps, for the last time under Rommel's eyes, attacked Montgomery at Medenine on March 6. For *Ultra's* role see Ralph Bennett's *Ultra and Mediterranean Strategy* [32]. *Ultra* gave fair strategic warning that a German counter-attack might be attempted, but it gave no hint of Rommel's battle plan.

Rommel's state of mind in this his last battle in Africa is discussed by David Fraser in his biography, *Knight's Cross: A Life of Field Marshal Erwin Rommel* [166]. Fraser notes that Rommel had inadequate forces and he was half-hearted. He had long decided that North Africa should be abandoned by the German-Italian forces.

Rommel repeated the worst mistakes of the earlier battle of Alam Halfa, and now the British had the new and powerful 17-pounder gun, as good as the German 88. Rommel abandoned the battle (Operation *Capri* to Rommel) by five o'clock in the afternoon of its first and only day. On March 9, Rommel handed over command of Army Group Africa to General von Arnim and flew to Rome. He would never see Africa again. Nigel Hamilton called the Battle of Medenine probably "the most immaculate brief defensive battle fought in World War II, the crowning laurel upon the head of Eighth Army."

Riding on the crest of success, Montgomery received a rude shock in the Battle of Mareth, March 20 to 27th. In his study, *Montgomery as Military Commander* [285], Ronald Lewin called the initial attack a "total and unmitigated failure." On the Mareth line the Axis forces were making their first serious stand since El Alamein, 1,500 miles away. Montgomery's *Memoirs* [337] are misleading since he gives the impression that the main attack was to be an outflanking movement.

In what is almost a model campaign study, *Crucible of Power: The Fight for Tunisia 1942-1943* [308], military historian Major Kenneth Macksey argues that Montgomery expected to break through the Mareth line with a frontal attack, and provided for only a weak encircling movement. When the frontal attack failed, Montgomery displayed his fundamental realism by closing down his frontal attack and reinforcing his outflanking movement. Macksey is also critical of Montgomery's conduct of the pursuit.

Montgomery's not uncritical biographer, Nigel Hamilton, thinks that fame, adulation and a growing feeling of infallibility after the Battle of Medenine all contributed to the Montgomery's dangerous over-confidence and the mistakes that he made in the Battle of Mareth.

General Francis Tuker's memoir, *Approach to Battle* [469] is also critical of the initial attack at Mareth. As befits the former commander of the 4th Indian Division, Tuker praises the bravery of the Madrassi and Sikh soldiers who calmly went about their mine-clearing task amidst the ear-splitting noise of battle and a hail of bullets.

General Jean Leclerc's Free French Force (included Senegalese troops) had served as part of Montgomery's outflanking force at Mareth (as did the Greek Sacred Squadron in some 30 jeeps mounted with machine guns). Henry Maule's, *Out of the Sand: The Epic Story of General Leclerc and the Fighting Free French* [322], recounts the remarkable feat of Leclerc's men who had marched 2,000 miles from Chad in central Africa to join the Allies.

Anthony Clayton focuses on the three courageous and successful French generals, Leclerc, Juin, and de Tassigny in his book, *Three Marshals of France: Leadership after Trauma* [97].

The official French history of the French Army in North Africa and the Free French in Tunisia, *La Campagne de Tunisie, 1942-1943* [438], by Marcel Spivak and Armand Leoni was published in 1985. Martin Blumenson has written that their account has "rescued the French units from obscurity and confusion."

In the Battle of Mareth, air-ground cooperation at long last became a reality. Francis De Guingand described how this came about in his memoir *Operation Victory*

[129]. The Desert Air Force became a flying artillery weapon under the innovative command of Air Vice-Marshal Harry Broadhurst. He even took up Montgomery's suggestion of hanging bombs onto fighter planes!

Italian General Giovanni Messe commanded the Axis army facing Montgomery's 8th Army. Messe's memoir, *Come Fini La Guerra in Africa: La "Prima Armata" Italiana in Tunisia* [327], is an important personal narrative. Messe commanded some very tough and determined Italian and German troops against the 8th Army. The last major battles on their part of the Tunisia front, at Wadi Akarit and Enfidaville, were as brutal as any fought in North Africa. New Zealand troops, including Maoris, figured prominently in both battles. The official New Zealand history, *Bardia to Enfidaville* [444] was written by W.G. Stevens. The Indian troops again fought magnificently. Their actions are described in the divisional history, *Fourth Indian Division* by G.R. Stevens. [443]. The fiercesome Gurkha troops wielded their deadly kukri knives in hand-to-hand combat with Axis soldiers. The 51st Highland Division also added laurels to their illustrious combat record.

As the Tunisian campaign came to a close, the "Flying Fortress" incident occurred in April 1943. Montgomery insisted on payment of a bet with Eisenhower that he would reach the Tunisian coastal plain by early April. The unwritten bet involved Eisenhower provided him with a B-17 plane and crew. Alanbrooke recorded the incident in his diary, and it appears in *The Turn of the Tide* (the Alanbrooke Papers) [65] edited by Arthur Byrant. Alanbrooke hauled Montgomery "over the coals" for upsetting Anglo-American relations. Montgomery had considered the matter great fun; Eisenhower did not.

ALEXANDER OF TUNIS

On February 20, 1943, General Sir Harold Alexander became Deputy Commander in Chief of the Allied Forces under Eisenhower, and Commander in Chief of 18th Army Group as well. That Army consisted of Anderson's First and Montgomery's 8th Armies, the U.S. II Corps, and Juin's French XIV Corps. His mission was to coordinate the Allied pincer movement in Tunisia and destroy the Axis forces. Three months later that mission was accomplished and Alexander would adopt the name "Tunis" for his peerage title after the war.

Alexander published his own memoirs in 1962 in response to Correlli Barnett's *The Desert Generals*. Extracts had earlier appeared in the London Sunday Times. *The Alexander Memoirs* [4] contained little that was new and did nothing to enhance his military reputation. His book was largely written by John North from Alexander's papers and diaries. Montgomery remarked that Alexander was "incapable of writing a book."

A shallow biography of Alexander was published in 1952 by Norman Hillson, *Alexander of Tunis: A Biographical Portrait* [213]. The work consisted mainly of anecdotes emphasizing his good qualities. Alexander was one of the least vain and egotistical World War II generals.

Alexander's military career was assessed by General W.G.F. Jackson in his book,

Alexander of Tunis as Military Commander [236]. While acknowledging that Alexander was "no Napoleon," the author admired him for his "calm" and "even-tempered" leadership. Unlike Montgomery, who carried the emotional baggage of a childhood starved of affection, Alexander had the personality of a relaxed, urbane patrician. Jackson recognized, however, Alexander's mistakes in his early dealings with Americans. Perhaps those mistakes were in part a result of his earlier unpleasant experience in Burma with General Joseph Stilwell who was not called "Vinegar Joe" for nothing.

In awe of his hero, Nigel Nicolson authored *The Life of Field Marshal Earl Alexander of Tunis* [353]. Very poorly documented, the study is by no means a definitive biography. Alexander was not a great strategist, but he inspired confidence and displayed legendary tact and patience in dealing with fiery subordinates; "Alex" has been termed the British Eisenhower in part became of his modesty and amiability.

Omar Bradley in his memoir, *A Soldier's Story* [54] had high praise for Alexander's "patient, wise, and fair-minded," leadership. He credits Alexander, more than anyone else, for helping the American army mature and come of age in Tunisia. Alexander was the Americans' favorite British general.

In his confidential reports in the aftermath of Kasserine, Alexander was extremely pessimistic about American fighting ability. The official U.S. Army history, *Northwest Africa: Seizing the Initiative in the West* [226] by George F. Howe observed that Alexander's unfavorable estimate was destined to linger, encouraging him to depend more heavily upon British units than later circumstances warranted.

Although the Americans' recovery from Kasserine was rapid and significant, it made virtually no impression on Alexander. In his well-written account, *World War II in the Mediterranean 1942-1945* [126], Carlo D'Este asserts that it was Alexander's easygoing amiability, and not his competence that established his rapport with the Americans. The author makes an even stronger case against Alexander in his acclaimed work, *Bitter Victory: The Battle for Sicily, 1943* [123]. Chapter II in that work is entitled, "Tunisia: The Testing Ground."

With more than a quarter of a million German and Italian soldiers surrounded in the small pocket round Tunis and Bizerta, all that remained of their African conquests, Alexander prepared to launch the climactic blow that would end the war in North Africa. In his initial plan, Operation *Strike*, Alexander gave II Corps just a token role by moving only one of its four divisions to the north, where it would "help" the First Army capture Bizerta. He did not reckon with American pride.

The American reaction to the attempt to squeeze them out of the final assault is decribed by Stephen E. Ambrose in *The Supreme Commander: The War Years of General Dwight D. Eisenhower* [5]. Bradley was "alarmed," Patton "exploded," and Eisenhower was "shocked." Eisenhower, keeping his temper, insisted that II Corps be given a more meaningful role. Alexander assigned them the capture of Bizerta.

The two accounts by Omar Bradley are both interesting sources for final American thrust on Bizerta: *A Soldier's Story* [54] and *A General's Life: An Autobiography* [55]. Blocking the American advance was what Bradley called the "massive hill" of Djebel Tahent or Hill 609 as it is better known. The five-day struggle for Hill 609 has become an American epic. At 2,000 feet, Hill 609 was the highest peak in the entire II Corps sector. The 34th Division captured the hill on April 30, and repelled furious German counterattacks. Previously criticized for its performance, the 34th Division went on to compile one of the best combat records in the American army.

On the British front, another celebrated Tunisian hill guarded the road to Tunis: Djebel El Almara earned fame as "Longstop Hill." From its heights, Tunis could be seen in the distance. In his eyewitness account, *African Trilogy* [339], war correspondent Alan Moorehead vividly described the battle for Longstop. After a terrible three-day battle, the British 78th Division took Longstop. Donkeys and mule teams had dragged ammunition and supplies to the men as they crept forward up the slopes of the mountain crests. Moorehead wrote of the survivors who reached the summit:"It was useless to picture these men who were winning the war for you as immaculate and shining young heroes agog with enthusiasm for the Cause. The had seen too much dirt and filth for that. . . They wanted to win and get out of it---the sooner the better. They had no high notions of glory."

On May 7, the U.S. 9th Division entered Bizerta. That same day, troops of the British 7th Armored Division entered Tunis, which soon gave itself up to song and dance. The French soldiers were nearly smoothered with kisses. Just after midnight on May 12/13, General Hans Cramer, the last commander of the famed *Deutsches Afrika Korps* (German Africa Corps), sent off his last signal to Germany:

Ammunition shot off. Arms and equipment destroyed. In accordance with orders received *D.A.K.* has fought itself to the condition where it can fight no more. The German Afrika Korps must rise again. Heia Safari. Cramer, General Commanding.

On May 12, General Jurgen von Arnim, commanding Army Group Africa, surrendered, as did General Giovanni Messe, commanding the Italian First Army, who was promoted Field Marshal that same day by Mussolini.

The following day, General Alexander signalled Churchill: "Sir, it is my duty to report that the Tunisian campaign is over. All enemy resistance has ceased. We are masters of the North African shores."

In his book, *Brute Force: Allied Strategy and Tactics in the Second World War* [145], author John Ellis is critical of what he terms the "extravagant claims made about the significance of the victory, both at the time and since." A different view is that taken by historian Gerhard L. Weinberg in his study, *A World At Arms: A Global History of World War II* [487], where he observed that some 275,000 German and Italian soldiers "walked, drove, or rode donkeys" into prisoner of war enclosures. It was the largest haul of Axis prisoners in the war to date. After witnessing the Victory Parade in Tunis on May 20, 1943, General Patton wrote in his memoir, "I hope this is only the first of many such triumphal processions in which I shall participate."

Besides an enemy army destroyed and the welding together of a closely-knit Allied command by General Eisenhower, the foundations had been laid for the American armies that would roll across Europe two years later. With the victory celebrations in Tunis behind them, the Allies prepared to take the next step in what Eisenhower would rightly call the *Crusade in Europe*.

8

Future Research

Few of the major campaigns of World War II campaigns aroused as much controversy as the War in North Africa, 1940-43. No other theater aroused such personal animosities. More than fifty years later, it is legitimate to ask, "What is there left to write about that three-year struggle in the desert and hills of North Africa?" Despite half-a-century of writing on the subject, however, there remain many gaps in the historical literature. Even the relative importance of the War in North Africa continues to be a source of dispute among historians and students of World War II. For some, a minor campaign that has received far too much attention, while to others North Africa is one of the most important theaters of World War II.

All too often, historical error has flowed down the channel of history like an unstoppable avalanche or glacier. In some Fiftieth Anniversary reflections on World War II, the distinguished historian Gerhard L. Weinberg declared that "scholars in all countries need to liberate their own minds and their own writings from a preoccupation with an enormous collection of dubious works and from the influence of an even larger mass of secondary works largely based on those memoirs." Weinberg's advice is particularly applicable to the writing on the North African war since so much of that literature has been marred by personality cults and blind partisanship.

Despite the gallons of ink spilt on the question of why an Allied North African campaign, an original, unbiased study, rooted in contemporary sources that considers all the issues and not just the military or logistical or any other single consideration involved in the decision, would not be a wasted effort. Likewise, Axis strategy would benefit from another look: Could "Plan Orient" have won the war? Were Rommel's strategic ideas realistic or fanciful? Since Martin Van Creveld's path-breaking work, *Supplying War*, there has been no further serious examination of the supply question. Was Hitler strategically correct to regard the Mediterranean as a secondary theater? Given Hitler's ideological goal of conquering living space in the East, is the previous question pointless? German historian Gerhard Schreiber of that country's outstanding Military History Research Office has argued that a Mediterranean strategy would have proved just a futile as the course Hitler actually pursued in the Soviet Union: A German conquest of the Middle East would have been meaningless since Britain's war effort was supported by the United States. Further research is needed before

Rommel's hopes and British fears for the loss of the Middle East are dismissed either as wishful thinking or as irrational fears.

Since the *Ultra* disclosures of the 1970s, and more especially since the publication in 1989 of Ralph Bennett's landmark study, *Ultra and Mediterranean Strategy*, a number of long-standing disputes involving Churchill, Auchinleck, and Montgomery have been largely resolved. The Prime Minister's constant prodding for action on the part of his desert commanders is at least in part understandable in light of the top secret information to which he was privy, thanks to *Ultra*. At the same time, although Churchill possessed *Ultra* information (not a foolproof guide) concerning German strength in North Africa, he did not understand his own Army's weaknesses. What exactly were the reasons for the British failure against Rommel? The officers background and training? Armored doctrine? Weapons? Up-to-date, deeply researched studies are needed on this question.

British generals have received most of the attention of biographers; few exist for German, Italian, or Dominion military leaders. If all historical writing is a progress report that represents a constant dialogue with the past, there is room for fresh assessments of even the most famous figures and their relationship to the North African war, from Roosevelt to Churchill. General George S. Patton, Jr., is the subject of a new biography by Carlo D'Este; Omar Bradley is awaiting a similar first-class study. Except for the Battle of Kasserine Pass and British accounts focusing on the 1st and 8th Armies, the relatively short but decisive Tunisian campaign when the American army came of age is awaiting a full-length study.

The Italian side of the hill has been presented by Lucio Ceva, Alberto Santoni, MacGregor Knox, and more recently by James Sadkovich, but far more research needs to be done in Italian-language sources.

Similarly, the subject of Vichy France as it relates to the war in North Africa is in need of further investigation. Why was the Vichy French army in North Africa willing and able to fight the Western Allies but not the Axis Powers? Not one German or Italian soldier was scratched when they landed in Tunisia; in contrast, hundreds of Americans were killed in French Morocco.

The battles that raged in North Africa half-a-century ago have receded into the distant past, and new generations have grown up with no personal or collective memory of what the world was like fifty years ago. If once closed military records, archival materials, and *Ultra* secrets are now available to the the researcher, the passage of time has its own historical pitfalls. The problem is that the researcher will lose touch with the reality of the past and completely fail to understand the problems faced by those who lived at the time. In a panel discussion on World War II scholarship, Michael Howard remarked that the main concern of historians today is not so much telling the story of what happened in the past, but recreating the mind-set of a past generation so as to help new generations to think, see, and feel in the way people of that time saw and felt. To understand, for example, why tears were shed when Tobruk surrendered in that grim summer of 1942.

The last World War II general, admiral and air marshal has written his memoirs. If most of these wartime participants attempted to tell their story honestly and truthfully, others distorted or misrepresented what happened, and in some cases, lied. This fact alone demands that historians confirm, revise, or refute what has previously been written. While the policies and decisions of the higher levels of command have received most of the attention of historians, there is a definite need to focus more attention on the attitudes, beliefs and ideas of the ordinary soldier. The oral and written history collections of World War II soldiers in the U.S. Army Military History Institute and the Imperial War Museum, as well as many other archives, are rich sources of historical information awaiting the attention of historians. In his Fiftieth Anniversary account, *El Alamein: Ultra and the Three Battles*, former infantryman Alexander Mckee related how many of his comrades had fought simply "to defend the bad against the worst." How common was this view? Far more research is needed to capture "the view from the foxhole."

Much splendid writing has been done on the three year war in North Africa, but there are gaps to be filled and endless questions to be asked and answered by new generations of students and historians.

Part II

BIBLIOGRAPHY

Bibliography

1.   Agar-Hamilton, John A. and L. C. F. Turner. *The Sidi Rezeg Battles, 1941.* London: Oxford University Press, 1957.

2.   Agar-Hamilton, John A. and L. C. F. Turner, eds. *Crisis in the Desert: May-July 1942.* London: Oxford University Press, 1952.

3.   Alexander, Field Marshal Earl. "The African Campaign from El Alamein to Tunis." Supplement to *The London Gazette*, February 5, 1948.

4.   Alexander, Field Marshal Earl. *The Alexander Memoirs.* edited by John North. London: Cassell, 1962.

5.   Ambrose, Stephen E. *Eisenhower.* Vol. 1. *Soldier, General of the Army, President-Elect 1890-1952.* New York: Simon and Schuster, 1983.

6.   Ambrose, Stephen E. *The Supreme Commander: The War Years of General Dwight D. Eisenhower.* London: Casssell, 1968.

7.   Andrew, Christopher and Jeremy Noakes, eds., *Intelligence and International Relations 1900-1945.* Exeter: University of Exeter, 1987.

8.   Ansel, Walter. *Hitler and the Middle Sea.* Durham: Duke University Press, 1972.

9.   Arnold, H. H. *Global Mission.* New York: Harper, 1949.

10.   Assman, Kurt. *Deutsche Schicksahlsjahre.* Wiesbaden: Brockhaus, 1950.

11.   Attard, Joseph. *The Battle of Malta.* London: Kimber, 1980.

12.   Atwater, William F. "United States Army and Navy Development of Joint Landing Operations, 1898-1942." Ph.D. diss., Duke University, 1986.

13. Auchinleck, Claude. "Operations in the Middle East from 1 November 1941 to 15 August 1942." Supplement to *The London Gazette*, 15 January 1948. Dispatch by Auchinlech. New Delhi: Govt. of India Press, 1943.

14. Auchinleck, Claude. "Operations in the Middle East from 5 July 1941 to 31 October 1941. Dispatch by Auchinlech. Published as a supplement to *The London Gazette*, 21 August 1946, 16 pp.

15. Austin, A. B. *Birth of an Army*. London: Gollancz, 1943.

16. Badoglio, Pietro. *Italy in the Second World War. Memories and Documents*. Westport, CT: Greenwood Press, 1976.

17. Baldwin, Hanson. *Battles Lost and Won: Great Campaigns of World War II*. New York: Harper & Row, 1966.

18. Barclay, Cyril N. *Against Great Odds: The Story of the First Offensive in Libya in 1940-41*. London: Blake and Mackenzie, 1955.

19. Barkas, Geoffrey. *The Camouflage Story (From Aintree to Alamein)*. London: Cassell, 1952.

20. Barker, A. J. *Afrika Korps*. London: Domus, 1978.

21. Barnett, Correlli. *Engage the Enemy More Closely: The Royal Navy in the Second World War*. New York: W. W. Norton, 1991.

22. Barnett, Correlli. *The Desert Generals*. 2nd ed. London: Allen and Unwin, 1983.

23. Barre, General Georges. *Tunisie, 1942-1943* Paris: Berger-Levrault, 1950.

24. Bates, Peter, *Dance of War: The Story of the Battle of Egypt*. London: Leo Cooper, 1992.

25. Baum, Walter and Eberhard Weichold. *Der Krieg der "Achsenmachte" im Mittelmeer-Raum: Die "Strategie" der Diktatoren*. (Studien und Dokumente zur Geschichte des Zweiten Weltkrieges, Nummber 14.) Gottingen: Muster-Schmidt. 1973.

26. Bayliss, Gwyn M. *Bibliographic Guide to the Two World Wars: An Annotated Survey of English-Language Reference Materials*. New York, 1978.

27. Baynes, John. *The Forgotten Victor: General Sir Richard O 'Connor.* London: Brassey's, 1989.

28. Beam, John C. "The Intelligence Background of Operation Torch," *Parameter*XIII (December 1983): 50-68.

29. Behrendt, Hans-Otts. *Rommel's Intelligence in the Desert Campaign, 1941-1943.* London: W. Kimber, 1985.

30. Behrens, C.B.A. *Merchant Shipping and the Demands of War.* London: Her Majesty's Stationery Office, 1955.

31. Belchem, David. *All in the Day's March.* London: Collins, 1978.

32. Bennett, Ralph Francis. *Ultra and Mediterranean Strategy.* New York: William Morrow, 1989.

33. Bergot, Erwan. *The Afrika Korps.* New York: Charter Books, 1976.

34. Bernotti, Admiral Romeo. *La Guerra sui Mari nel Conflitto Mondiale.* Livorno: Societa Editrice Tirrena, 1948.

35. Bernstein, B. L. *Tide Turned at Alamein: Impressions of the Desert War with the South African Division and the Eighth Army, June 1941-January, 1943.* Johannesburg: Central News Agency, 1944.

36. Beurling, George F. and Leslie Roberts. *Malta Spitfire.* New York: Farrar, 1943.

37. Beus, Jacobus Gitsbertus de. *Formorrow at Dawn!* New York: Norton, 1979.

38. Bharucha, P. C. *The North African Campaign, 1940-1943, Official History of the Indian Armed Forces in the Second World* War. Calcutta: Combined Inter-Services, Historical Section, 1956.

39. Bidwell, Shelford and Dominick Graham. *Fire-Power: British Army Weapons and Theories of War 1904-1945.* Boston: George Allen and Unwin, 1985.

40. Bidwell, Shelford. *Gunners at War: A Tactical study of the Royal Artillery in the Twentieth Century.* London: Arms & Armour Press, 1970.

41. Bingham, James K. W. and Werner Kaupt. *The North African Campaign, 1940-1943.* Trans. by K. Kirkness. London: MacDonald, 1969.

42. Blamey, A. E. *A Company Commander Remembers: From El Yibo to El Alamein.* Pietermaritzburg: Natal Witness, 1963.

43. Blanco, Richard L. *Rommel, the Desert Warrior: The Afrika Korps in World War II.* New York: Julian Messner, 1982.

44. Blaxland, Gregory. *The Plain Cook and the Great Showman: The First and Eighth Armies in North Africa.* London: William Kimber, 1977.

45. Blumenson, Martin. *Kasserine Pass.* Boston: Houghton Mifflin, 1967.

46. Blumenson, Martin. *Mark Clark: The Last of the Great World War II Commanders.* New York: Congdon & Weed, 1984.

47. Blumenson, Martin. *Patton: The Man Behind the Legend 1885-1945.* New York: Morrow, 1986.

48. Blumenson, Martin. *The Patton Papers, 1940-1945.* Boston: Houghton Mifflin, 1974.

49. Bongiovanni, Alberto. *Battaglie Nel Deserto: Da Sidi El-Barran a El Alamein.* Milan: Mursia, 1978.

50. Borgiotti, Alberto and Cesare Gori. *La guerra aerea in Africa settentrionale: Assalto dal cielo 1940-41; 1942-43.* in two volumes. Modena: S.T.E.M.-Mucchi s.p.a. 1972; 1973.

51. Bowyer, Chaz and Christopher Shores, *Desert Air Force at War.* London: Ian Allan, 1980.

52. Braddock, David W. *The Campaigns in Egypt and Libya, 1940-1942.* Aldershot: Gale and Polken, 1964.

53. Bradford, Ernle. *Siege: Malta 1940-1943.* New York: William Morrow, 1986.

54. Bradley, Omar N. *A Soldier's Story.* New York: Henry Holt, 1951.

55. Bradley, Omar N. and Clay Blair. *A General's Life: An Autobiography.* New York: Simon and Schuster, 1983.

56. Bragadin, Marc' Antonio. *The Italian Navy in World War II.* Annapolis, Md: U.S. Naval Institute, 1957.

57. Brett-James, Antony. *Ball of Fire: The Fifth Indian Division in the Second World War*. Aldershot: Gale and Polden, 1951.

58. Brett-James, Antony. *Conversations with Montgomery*. London: W. Kimber, 1984.

59. Breuer, William B. *Operation Torch: The Allied Gamble to Invade North Africa*. New York: St. Martin's, 1985.

60. Brooks, Russell, "Casablanca--the French Side of the Fence." *U.S. Naval Institute Proceedings*, 77 (Sept. 1951): 909-25.

61. Brooks, Stephen, ed. *Montgomery and the Eighth Army: A Selection from the Diaries, Correspondence and other Papers of Field Marshal The Viscount Montgomery of Alamein, August 1942 to December 1943*. London: The Army Records Society, 1991.

62. Brown, James Ambrose. *One Man's War: A Soldier's Diary*. Sparta, NJ: H. Timmins, 1980.

63. Brownlow, Donald G. *Checkmate at Ruweisat: Auchinleck's Finest Hour*. North Quincy, MA: Christopher Pub. House, 1977.

64. Bryant, Arthur, ed. *The Alanbrooke War Diaries*. Vol. 1, *The Turn of the Tide*. London: Collins, 1957.

65. Bryant, Arthur, ed. *The Alanbrooke War Diaries*. Vol. II. *Triumph in the West*. London: Collins, 1959.

66. Burdick, Charles. *Unternehmen Sonnenblume*. Neckargemund: Kurt Vowinckel Verlag, 1980.

67. Butcher, Harry C. *My Three Years with Eisenhower: The Personal Diary of Captain Harry C. Butcher*. New York: Simon & Schuster, 1946.

68. Butler, J. R. M. *Grand Strategy*. Vol. III, Part II, *June 1941-August 1942*. London: Her Majesty's Stationery Office, 1961.

69. Caccia Dominioni de Sillavengo, Paolo. *Alamein 1933-1962: An Italian Story*. Trans. by Dennis Chamberlin.. London: Allen & Unwin, 1966.

70. Cameron, Ian. *Red Duster, White Ensign: The Story of the Malta Convoys*. London: Frederick Muller, 1959.

71. Cannistraro, Philip V.,ed. *Historical Dictionary of Fascist Italy*. Westport, CT: Greenwood Press, 1982.

72. Carell, Paul. *The Foxes of the Desert*. Trans from German by Mervyn Savill. New York: E. P. Dutton, 1961.

73. Carlton, David. *Anthony Eden: A Biography*. London: A. Lane, 1981.

74. Carmichael, Thomas N. *The Ninety Days*. New York: Geis, 1971.

75. Carrington, Charles. *Soldier at Bomber Command*. London: Leo Cooper, 1987.

76. Carver, Michael, ed. *The War Lords: Military Commanders of the Twentieth Century*. Boston: Little Brown, 1976.

77. Carver, Michael. *Dilemmas of the Desert War: A New Look at the Libyan Campaign, 1940-1942*. Bloomington: Indiana University Press, 1986.

78. Carver, Michael. *El Alamein*. New York: The Macmillan Co., 1962.

79. Carver, Michael. *Harding of Petherton*. London: Weidenfeld & Nicolson, 1978.

80. Carver, Michael. "Review of Roger Parkinson's *The Auk*," *Times Literary Supplement*, November 4, 1977, p. 1289.

81. Carver, Michael. *Tobruk*. Philadelphia: DuFour Editions, 1964.

82. Cavallero, Ugo. *Comando Supremo. Diario 1940-1943 Del Capo Di S.M.G.* Bologna: Cappaelli, 1948.

83. Ceva, Lucio. "The North African Campaign, 1940-43: A Reconsideration," *Journal of Strategic Studies* (Great Britain), 13, No. 1 (1990).

84. Ceva, Lucio. *Africa Settentrionale 1940-1943*. Rome: Bonacci Editore, 1982.

85. Ceva, Lucio. *La Condotta Italiana Della Guerra Cavallero E Il Comando Supremo, 1941-1942*. Milan: Feltrinelli, 1975.

86. Chalfont, Alun. *Montgomery of Alamein*. New York: Atheneum, 1976.

87. Chandler, Alfred D., Jr., ed., and Stephen E. Ambrose, assoc. ed. *The Papers of Dwight David Eisenhower: The War Years*. 5 vols. Baltimore: The Johns Hopkins Press, 1967.

88. Chant, Christopher. *The Encyclopedia of Code Names of World War II.*

89. Charmley, John. *Churchill: The End of Glory, A Political Biography.* New York: Harcourt, Brace, 1993.

90. Churchill, Winston. *The Second World War.* Vol II, *Their Finest Hour.* London: Cassell, 1949.

91. Churchill, Winston. *The Second World War.* Vol. III, *The Grand Alliance.* London, Cassell, 1950.

92. Churchill, Winston. *The Second World War.* Vol. IV, *The Hinge of Fate.* London: Cassell, 1951.

93. Ciano, Count Galeazzo. *The Ciano Diaries, 1939-1943.* Garden City, NY: Doubleday, 1946.

94. Clark, Mark W. *Calculated Risk.* New York: Harper & Brothers, 1950.

95. Clark, Ronald William. *Montgomery of Alamein.* London: Phoenix House, 1960.

96. Clay, Ewart W. *The Path of the 50th: The Story of the 50th (Northumbrian) Division in the Second World War, 1939-1945.* Aldershot:Gale and Polden, 1950.

97. Clayton, Anthony. *Three Marshals of France: Leadership After Trauma.* London: Brassey's, 1992.

98. Clifford, Alexander. *The Conquest of North Africa, 1940-1943.* Boston: Little, Brown, 1943.

99. Cline, Ray S. *Washington Command Post: The Operations Division.* Washington, DC: Department of the Army, 1951.

100. Coats, Peter. *Of Generals and Gardens: The Autobiography of Peter Coats.* London: Weidenfeld, 1968.

101. Cocchia, Aldo. *La Marina Italiana nella Seconda Guerra Mondiale.* Rome: State Maggiore, 1958.

102. Coffin, Howard Macy. *Malta Story.* Based on the diary and experiences of H. M. Coffin by W. L. River. New York: Dutton, 1943.

103. Coggins, Jack. *The Campaign for North Africa.* Garden City, NY: Doubleday, 1980.

104. Colacicchi, Paolo. *L'ultimo fronte d'Africa: Tunisia*, Novembre 1942-Maggio 1943. Milan: Mursia, 1977.

105. Coles, Harry L. *Ninth Air Force in the Western Desert Campaign to 23 January 1943.* Washington, DC: AAF Historical Division, 1945.

106. Collins, R. J. *Lord Wavell.* London, 1947.

107. Connell, John. *Auchinleck: A Biography of Field Marshal Sir Claude Auchinleck.* London: Cassell, 1959.

108. Connell, John. *Wavell: Scholar and Soldier.* New York: Harcourt , Brace, 1965.

109. Cooling, Benjamin Franklin. *Case Studies in the Development of Close Air Support.* Washington, DC: Office of Air Force History, 1990.

110. Coon, Carleton S. *A North African Story: The Anthropologist as OSS Agent 1941-1943.* Ipswich, Mass.: Gambit, 1980.

111. Cooper, Martin. *The German Army 1933-45: Its Political and Military Failure.* London: Macdonald & Jane's, 1978.

112. Cordier, Sherwood S. "Alam Halfa--Last Chance in North Africa." *Military Review.* 50, No. 11 (1970): 62-74.

113. Cordier, Sherwood Stanley. *Erwin Rommel as Commander: The Decisive Years, 1940-1942.* Ph.D. diss., U. of Minnesota, 1963.

114. Coutau-Begarie, Hervé and Claude Huan, *Darlan.* Paris: Fayard, 1989.

115. Coward, Noel. *Middle East Diary.* New York: Doubleday Doran, 1944.

116. Cox, Geoffrey. *A Tale of Two Battles: A Personal Memoir of Crete and the Western Desert 1941.* London: Kimber, 1987.

117. Craven, Wesley Frank and James Lea Cate, *The Army Air Forces in World War Two.* Vol. II. *Europe: Torch to Pointblank, August 1942 to December 1943.* Washington, DC: Office of Air Force History, 1983. (Originally published 1949 by The University of Chicago.)

118. Crisp, Robert. *Brazen Chariots: An Account of Tank Warfare in the Western Desert, November-December 1941.* Foreword by Lord Harding. London: Muller, 1959.

119. Crosskill, W. E. *The Two Thousand Mile War*. London: R. Hale, 1980.

120. Cruickshank, Charles. *Deception in World War II*. New York: Oxford University Press, 1979.

121. Cunningham, Andrew Browne. *A Sailor's Odyssey. The Autobiography of Admiral of the Fleet Viscount Cunningham of Hyndhope*. London: Hutchinson, 1951.

122. D'Arcy-Dawson, John. *Tunisian Battle*. London: MacDonald, 1943.

123. D'Este, Carlo. *Bitter Victory: The Battle for Sicily July-August 1943*. New York: Harper, 1991.

124. D'Este, Carlo W. *Patton: A Genius For War*. New York: Harper Collins, 1995.

125. D'Este, Carlo. "Review of *Brute Force* by John Ellis," *Journal of Military History* 55, no. 2 (April 1991): 266-67.

126. D'Este, Carlo. *World War II in the Mediterranean 1942-1945*. Chapel Hill, NC: Algonquin Books, 1990.

127. Danchev, Alex. *Establishing the Anglo-American Alliance: The Second World War Diaries of Brigadier Vivian Dykes*. New York: Brassey's, 1990.

128. De Belot, Raymond. *The Struggle for the Mediterranean 1939-1945*. Trans. by James A. Field, Jr. Princeton, NJ: Princeton University Press, 1951.

129. De Guingand, Sir Francis. *Operation Victory*. New York: Charles Scribner's, 1947.

130. De Gaulle, Charles. *The War Memoirs of Charles de Gaulle*. 2 vols. New York: Simon and Schuster, 1959.

131. *Desert Victory*. Film produced by Army Film and Photographic Unit and Royal Air Force Film Production Unit. Chicago: Questar/Travel Network, 1989.

132. Deutsch, Harold C. "Commanding Generals and the Uses of Intelligence," *Intelligence and National Security* 3, no. 3 (1988): 194-260.

133. *Diamond Track: From Egypt to Tunisia with the Second New Zealand Division, 1942-1943*. Wellington: New Zealand Army Board, 1945.

134. Dick, Bernard F. *The American World War II Film.* Lexington, KY: University of Kentucky Press, 1985.

135. Divine, A. D. *The Road to Tunis.* London: Collins, 1944.

136. Dornbusch, Charles E. *Unit Histories, Personal Narratives, United States Army: A Checklist.*

137. Dougherty, James J. *The Politics of Wartime Aid: American Economic Assistance to France and French Northwest Africa, 1940-1946.* (Contributions in American History, number 71) Westport, Conn.: Greenwood Press, 1978.

138. Douglas, Keith. *Alamein to Zem Zem.* London: Faber, 1946.

139. Douglas-Hamilton, James. *The Air Battle for Malta.* Edinburgh: Mainstream, 1981.

140. Dupuy, R. Ernest and Trevor N. Dupuy. *The Encyclopedia of Military History: From 3500 B.C. to the Present.*

141. Dupuy, Trevor N. *The Halder Diaries: The Private War Journals of Colonel General Franz Halder.* Boulder, CO: Westview Press, 1976.

142. Eisenhower, Dwight D. *Letters to Mamie.* ed. John S. D. Eisenhower. Garden City, NY: Doubleday, 1978.

143. Eisenhower, Dwight D. *Crusade in Europe.* New York: Doubleday, 1948.

144. Eisenhower, John S. D. *Allies: Pearl Harbor to D-Day.* Garden City, NY: Doubleday, 1982.

145. Ellis, John. *Brute Force: Allied Strategy and Tactics in the Second World War.* New York: Viking, 1990.

146. Ellsberg, Edward. *No Banners, No Bugles.* New York: Dodd, Mead, 1955.

147. Enser, A. G. S. *A Subject Bibliography of the Second World War: Books in English, 1939-1974.* Boulder, Co.

148. Enser, A. G. S. *A Subject Bibliography of the Second World War: Books in English, 1975-1983.* Boulder, Co.

149. Esebeck, Hanns-Gert Von. *Das Deutsche Afrika-Korps.* Wiesbaden: Limes Verlags, 1975.

150. Esposito, Vincent J. *The West Point Atlas of American Wars. Vol. II, 1900-1953.* New York, 1959.

151. Essame, H. *Patton A Study in Command.* New York: Charles Scribner's Sons, 1974.

152. Ethell, Jeff. "'Lightning over Africa': The Story of America's Versatile and Durable P-38 During WW-II Action Over North Africa," *Aviation Quarterly* 5, No. 1 (1979): 88-104.

153. Farago, Ladislas. *Patton: Ordeal and Triumph.* New York: Astor-Honor, 1964.

154. Farrar-Hockley, Anthony. *The War in the Desert.* London: Faber & Faber, 1969.

155. Ferris, John. "Ralph Bennett and the Study of Ultra," *Intelligence and National Security*, Vol. 6, no. 2 (April 1991): 473-86.

156. Ferris, John. "The British Army, Signals and Security in the Desert Campaign, 1940-42," *Intelligence and National Security*, Vol. 5, No. 2 (April 1990): 255-87.

157. Findlay, Allan M., Anne M. Findlay, and Richard I. Lawless. *Tunisia.* Santa Barbara, Ca.: World Bibliographic Series, Clio Press.

158. Fink, Carole, Isabel V. Hull and MacGregor Knox, eds. *German Nationalism and the European Response, 1890-1945.* Norman, OK: University of Oklahoma Press, 1985.

159. Fisher, John O. H. *Montgomery of Alamein: The General Who Never Lost a Campaign.* London: Hodder and Stoughton, 1981.

160. Fisher, Nigel. *Harold MacMillan, a Biography.* New York: St. Martin's Press, 1982.

161. Forty, George. *Desert Rats at War: North Africa.* London: Ian Allan, 1975.

162. Forty, George. *Tanks Across the Desert: The War Diary of Jake Wardrop.* London: Kimber, 1981.

163. Forty, George. *The First Victory: General O'Connor's Desert Triumph, Dec. 1940 - Feb. 1941.* Tunbridge, Wales: Nutshell, 1990.

164. Foster, Janet and Julia Sheppard. *British Archives: a Guide to Archive Resources in the United Kingdom.* New York, 1989.

165. Fraser, David. *Alanbrooke*. With a prologue and epilogue by Arthur Bryant. New York: Atheneum, 1982.

166. Fraser, David. *Knight's Cross: A Life of Field Marshal Erwin Rommel.* London: Harper Collins, 1993.

167. Freidin, Seymour, ed. *The Fatal Decisions*. London: M. Joseph, 1956.

168. Fuller, J. F. C. *The Second World War*. London: Eyre & Spottiswoode, 1948.

169. Funk, Arthur L. *The Second World War: A Select Bibliography of Books in English Published Since 1975.* Claremont, CA: Regina, 1985.

170. Funk, Arthur L. *The Second World War: A Select Bibliography of Books in English 1980-1984.* Gainesville, FL, 1984.

171. Funk, Arthur Layton. *The Politics of TORCH:The Allied Landings and the Algiers Putsch, 1942.* Lawrence, KS: The University Press of Kansas, 1974.

172. Fussell, Paul, ed. *The Norton Book of Modern War*. New York: W. W. Norton, 1991.

173. Fyne, Robert. *The Hollywood Propaganda of World War II*. Metachen, NJ: The Scarecrow Press, 1994.

174. Gabriele, Mariano. *Operazione C 3: Malta*. Rome: Ufficio Storico della Marina Militaire, 1965.

175. Gelb, Norman. *Desperate Venture: The Story of Operation Torch, the Allied Invasion of North Africa*. New York: William Morrow, 1992.

176. Giamberardino, Oscar Di. *La marina nella tragedia nazionale*. Rome: Polin, 1945.

177. Gilbert, Martin. *Winston S. Churchill: Finest Hour*. Vol. VI. Boston: Houghton Mifflin, 1983.

178. Gilbert, Martin. *Winston S. Churchill: Road to Victory*. Vol. VII. Boston: Houghton Mifflin, 1986.

179. Gill, G. Hermon. *Royal Australian Navy, 1939-1942*. Canberra: Australian War Memorial, 1957.

180. Gill, G. Hermon. *Royal Australian Navy, 1942-1945*. Canberra: Australian War Memorial, 1958.

181. Gillison, Douglas. *Royal Australian Air Force, 1939-1942.* Canberra: Australian War Memorial, 1962.

182. Godson, Susan H. *Viking of Assault: Admiral John Leslie Hall, Jr. and Amphibious Warfare.* Washington, DC: University Press of America, 1982.

183. Gooch, John, ed. *Decisive Campaigns of the Second World War.* London: F. Cass, 1990.

184. Gooch, John. "Italian Military Competence," *The Journal of Strategic Studies,* no. 2 (June 1982): 256-65.

185. Gordon, John W. *The Other Desert War: British Special Forces in North Africa, 1940-1943.* Westport, CT: Greenwood, 1987.

186. Gosset, Renee P. *Conspiracy in Algiers: 1942-1943.* translated from French. New York: Narion Assoc., 1945.

187. Greacen, Lavinia. *Chink: A Biography.* London: Macmillan, 1989.

188. Green, David M. "El Alamein, '89," *After the Battle* 68 (1990): 48-53.

189. Greene, Jack and Alessandro Massignani. *Rommel's North African Campaign, September 1940-November 1942.* Conshohocken, PA: Combined Books, 1994

190. Greenfield, George. *Desert Episode.* London: Macmillan, 1945.

191. Greiss. *Campaign Atlas to the Second World War.* Wayne, NJ., 1989.

192. Griffith, Paddy. *Battle Tactics of the Western Front: The British Army's Art of Attack, 1916-18.* New Haven: Yale, 1994

193. Grimley, Edmund. *The Big Six: Montgomery, Eisenhower, Tedder, Ramsay, Leigh-Mallory, Bradley.* With a Foreword by Major Sir Jocelyn Jones, M.P. London: Alliance Press Limited, 1944.

194. Guedalla, Philip. *Middle East 1940-1942: A Study in Air Power.* London: Hodder & Stoughton, 1944.

195. Hall, Timothy, *Tobruk 1941:The Desert Siege.* North Ryde, Australia: Methuen, 1984.

196. Hallion, Richard P. *Strike From the Sky: The History of Battlefield Air Attack, 1911-1945.* Washington, DC: Smithsonian Institution Press, 1989.

197. Halton, Matthew H. *Ten Years to Alamein.* London: Drummond, 1944.

198. Hamilton, Nigel. *Master of the Battlefield: Monty's War Years 1942-1944.* New York: McGraw-Hill, 1983.

199. Hamilton, Nigel. *Monty: The Final Years of the Field-Marshal, 1944-1976.* New York: McGraw-Hill, 1987.

200. Hamilton, Nigel. *Monty: The Making of a General 1887-1942.* New York: McGraw-Hill, 1981.

201. Hammond, Keith. "Rommel: Aspects of the Man." *Army Quarterly and Defence Journal,* 112, No. 4 (1982): 472-76.

202. Harmon, Ernest N. *Combat Commander: Autobiography of a Soldier.* Englewood Cliffs,NJ: Prentice-Hall, 1970.

203. Harouni, Brahim. "How the Anglo-American Invasion of North Africa in November 1942 was Prepared and Realized." Ph.D. diss., University of Reading, England, 1987.

204. Heckmann, Wolf. *Rommel's War in Africa.* Garden City, N.Y.: Doubleday, 1981.

205. Heckstall-Smith, Anthony. *Tobruk.* New York: W. W. Norton, 1960.

206. Henderson, Hamish. *Elegies for the Dead in Cyrenaica.* Edinborgh: EUSPB, 1948.

207. Hewitt, H. Kent. "The Landing in Morocco November 1942." *United States Naval Institute Proceedings* 78 (Nov. 1952): 1242-53.

208. Hibbert, Christopher. *Mussolini.* New York: Ballantine Books, 1972.

209. Higham, Robin and Donald J. Mrozek. *A Guide to the Sources in U. S. Military History: Supplement III.* Hamden, CT, 1993.

210. Hill, L. Gordon, Jr. "Rommel: Fox or Fake?" *Marine Corps Gazette* 45, no. 6 (1961): 26-31.

211. Hill, Russell. *Desert War.* New York: A. A. Knopf, 1942.

212. Hillgruber, Andreas. *Hitler's Strategie, Politik, Kriegfuhrung, 1939-1941.* Frankfurt: Bernard & Graefe, 1967.

213. Hillson, Noman. *Alexander of Tunis: A Biographical Portrait.* London: Allen, 1952.

214. Hinsley, F. H. and Alan Stripp, eds., *Codebreakers.* Oxford: Oxford University Press, 1993.

215. Hinsley, F. H. *British Intelligence in the Second World War: Its Influence on Strategy and Operations.* Vol. II. Part VI, *The Mediterranean and North Africa from July 1941 to January 1943.* New York: Cambridge University Press, 1981.

216. Holden, Matthew. *The Desert Rats.* London: Wayland Publishers, 1973.

217. Holmes, Richard. *Bir Hakeim: Desert Citadel.* New York: Ballantine Books, 1971.

218. Horner, D. M. *High Command: Australia and Allied Strategy 1939-1945.* Canberra: Australian War Memorial, 1982.

219. Horner, D. M., ed., *The Commanders, Australian Military Leadership in the Twentieth Century.* Sydney: George Allen & Unwin, 1984.

220. Horrocks, General Sir Brian. *A Full Life.* London: Collins, 1960.

221. Horsfield, John. *The Art of Leadership in War: The Royal Navy from the Age of Nelson to the End of World War II.* Westport, CT: Greenwood Press, 1980.

222. Howard, Michael. *Grand Strategy,* Vol. IV, *August 1942-September 1943.* London: Her Majesty's Stationery Office, 1972.

223. Howard, Michael. *The Causes of Wars and Other Essays.* London: Temple Smith, 1983.

224. Howard, Michael. *The Mediterranean Strategy in the Second World War.* London: Weidenfield and Nicolson, 1968.

225. Howarth, T. E. B., ed. *Monty at Close Quarters: Recollections of the Man.* London: Chivers, 1987.

226. Howe, George F. *Northwest Africa: Seizing the Initiative in the West.* United States Army in World War II. Washington, DC: Department of the Army, 1957.

227. Howe, George F. *The Battle History of the 1st Armored Division, "Old Ironsides."* Washington, DC: Combat Forces Press, 1954.

228. Humble, Richard. *Crusader: The Eighth Army's Forgotten Victory, November 1941-January 1942*. London: Leo Cooper, 1987.

229. Hunt, David. *A Don at War*. London: Frank Cass, 1990. (Original edition 1966).

230. Iachino, Angelo. *Gaudo e Matapan; Storia di un operazione della guerra navale nel Mediterraneo, 27-28-29 Marzo 1941*. Milan: Mondadori, 1946.

231, Infield, Glenn B. *Disaster at Bari*. New York: Macmillan, 1971.

232. Irving, David, ed. *Papers Relating to the Allied High Command, 1943-46*. Wakefield, West Yorkshire, England: Microform, Ltd., 1983. Microfilm.

233. Irving, David. *The Trail of the Fox: The Life of Field-Marshal Erwin Rommel*. New York: E. P. Dutton, 1977.

234. Ismay, H. L. *Memoirs*. London: Viking, 1960.

235. Jablonski, David. *The Desert Warriors*. New York: Lancer Books, 1972.

236. Jackson, W. G. F. *Alexander of Tunis As Military Commander*. London: Batsford, 1971.

237. Jackson, W. G. F. *The Battle for North Africa 1940-43*. New York: Mason/Charter, 1975.

238. Jacob, A. *A Traveller's War: A Journey to the Wars in Africa, India and Russia*. London: Collins, 1944.

239. Jacobs, W. A. "Air Support for the British Army, 1939-1943," *Military Affairs*. XLV (December 1982).

240. Jacobsen, H. A. and J. Rohwer, eds. *Decisive Battles of World War Two: The German View*. New York: G. P. Putnam's Sons, 1965.

241. James, Malcolm. *Born of the Desert: With the SAS in North Africa*. California: Presidio Press, 1991.

242. James, Meyrich Edward Clifton. *I Was Monty's Double*. London: Popular Book Club, 1954.

243. James, Meyrich Edward Clifton. *I Was Monty's Double*. Screenplay by Bryan Forbes. Janus Films, 1986. Videocassette.

244. Jellison, Charles A. *Besieged: The World War II Ordeal of Malta, 1940-1942.* Hanover, NH: University Press of New England, 1984.

245. Jewell, Derek, ed. *Alamein and the Desert War.* New York: Ballantine, 1967.

246. Jewell, N. L. A. *Secret Submarine Mission.* New York: Ziff-Davis Publishing, 1944.

247. Jones, Vincent. *Operation Torch: Anglo-American Invasion of North Africa.* New York: Ballantine Books, 1972.

248. Jordan, Gerald. *British Military History: A Supplement to Robin Higham's Guide to the Sources.* New York, 1988.

249. Jordan, Philip Furneaux. *Jordan's Tunis Diary.* London: Collins, 1943.

250. Juin, Marshal Alphonse. *Memoires.* Paris: Artheme Fayard, 1959.

251. Kay, R. L. *Long Range Desert Group in Libya, 1940-41.* Wellington:: War History Branch, 1949.

252. Kay, R. L. *Long Range Desert Group in the Mediterranean.* Wellington: War History Branch, 1950.

253. Keefer, Louis E., *Italian Prisoners of War in America 1942-1946.* New York: Praeger, 1992.

254. Keegan, John, ed. *Churchill's Generals.* New York: Grove Weidenfeld, 1991.

255. Keegan, John. *Encyclopedia of World War II.* London: Hamlyn, 1977.

256. Keegan, John. *The Times Atlas of the Second World War.* New York: Harper & Row, 1989.

257. Keegan, John. *Who Was Who in World War II.* New York, Crowell, 1978.

258. Kennedy, General Sir James. *The Business of War.* London: Hutchinson, 1957.

259. Kershaw, Andrew and Ian Close, eds. *The Desert War.* London: Phoebus, 1975.

260. Kesselring, Albert. *The Memoirs of Field Marshal Kesselring.* Novato, CA: Presidio Press, 1989.

261. Kielar, Eugenia J. *Thank You Uncle Sam: Letters of a World War II Army*

Nurse from North Africa and Italy. Bryn Mawr, PA: Dorrance & Co., 1987.

262. Kimball, Warren F. *Churchill and Roosevelt, the Complete Correspondence.* Vol. II, *Alliance Forged, November 1942-February 1944.* Princeton: Princeton University Press, 1984.

263. King, Ernest J. and Walter M. Whitehill, *Fleet Admiral King: A Naval Record.* New York: Norton, 1952.

264. Kinghorn, Alan. *The Dynamic War: A Study in Military Leadership in the British-German Campaigns in North Africa, February 1941-January 1943.* New York: Exposition-University Press, 1970.

265. Kingseed, Cole C., "Review Essay: World War II Desert Warfare." *Military Review* 71, no. 2 (1991): 79-81.

266. Kippenberger, H. K. *Infantry Brigadier.* New York: Oxford University Press, 1949.

267. Kirk, Alan G. *Oral History of ADM Alan G. Kirk, USN.* Edited by Columbia University Oral History Research Office. New York: Columbia University, 1888-1945 (microfiche).

268. Kirkland, Donald E. *Rommel's Desert Campaigns.* Fort Leavenworth, KS: U.S. Army Command and General Staff College, 1986.

269. Kirkpatrick, Charles. "Joint Planning for Operation Torch," *Parameters XXI* (Summer 1991).

270. Knickerbocker, H. R., et al. *Danger Forward: The Story of the First division in World War II.* Washington, DC: Society of the First Division, 1947.

271. Knox, MacGregor. *Mussolini Unleashed, 1939-1941: Politics and Strategy in Fascist Italy's Last War.* New York: Cambridge University Press, 1982.

272. Koeltz, General Louis. *Une Campagne Que Nous Avons Gagnée.* Paris: Hachette, 1959.

273. Koenig, Pierre Joseph. *Bir Hakeim.* Paris: Realités, 1951.

274. Kogan, Norman. *Italy and the Allies.* Westport, CT: Greenwood Press, 1982.

275. Kuhn, Volkmar. *Rommel in the Desert: Victories and Defeat of the Afrika Korps, 1941-1943.* West Chester, PA: Schiffer, 1991.

276. Kuter, Laurence S. "Goddammit, Georgie!" *Air Force Magazine* 56, no. 2 (1973): 51-56.

277. Landsborough, Gordon. *Tobruk Commando.* New York: Avon, 1958.

278. Lane, Ann. "The Inevitable Victory? El Alamein Revisited," *Imperial War Museum Review,* No. 7 (1993): 83-87.

279. Langhorne, Richard, ed., *Diplomcy and Intelligence During the Second World War: Essays in Honour of F. H. Hinsley.* New York: Cambridge University Press, 1985.

280. Lawlor, Sheila. *Churchill and the Politics of War, 1940-1941.* New York: Cambridge University Press, 1994.

281. Leahy, William. *I Was There: The Personal Story of the Chief of Staff to Presidents Roosevelt and Truman.* New York: Whittlesay House, 1950.

282. Leighton, Richard M. and R. W. Coakley. *Global Logistics and Strategy, 1940-1943.* Washington, DC: Department of the Army, 1968

283. Lewin, Ronald. *Hitler's Mistakes.* London: Cooper, 1984

284. Lewin, Ronald. *Life and Death of the Afrika Korps.* London: Batsford, 1977.

285. Lewin, Ronald. *Montgomery as Military Commander.* New York: Stein and Day, 1971.

286. Lewin, Ronald. *Rommel as Military Commander.* London: Batsford, 1968.

287. Lewin, Ronald. *The Chief: Field Marshal Lord Wavell, Commander-in-Chief and Viceroy, 1939-1947.* New York: Farrar Straus, Giroux, 1981.

288. Liddell Hart, B.H. "How Hitler Missed in the Middle East," *Marine Corps Gazette* 40, no. 11 (1956): 50-54.

289. Liddell Hart, B. H. *The German Generals Talk.* New York: William Morrow, 1948.

290. Liddell Hart, B. H. *The Other Side of the Hill: Germany's Generals, Their Rise and Fall, with Their Own Account of Military Events, 1939-1940.* London: Macmillan, 1993.

291. Lloyd, Air Marshal Sir Hugh. *Briefed to Attack*. London: Hodder and Staughton, 1949.

292. Lochner, Louis P. ed. and trans. *The Goebbels Diaries, 1942-1943*. New York: 1948.

293. Long, G. *To Bengazi*. Canberra: Australian War Memorial, 1953.

294. Long, Gavin. *The Final Campaigns*. Canberra: Australian War Memorial, 1963.

295. Longmore, Arthur M. *From Sea to Sky, 1910-1945*. London: G. Bles, 1946.

296. Lucas, James S. *War in the Desert: the Eighth Army at El Alamein*. New York: Beufort, 1982.

297. Lucas, James. *Panzer Army Africa*. London: MacDonald and Jane's, 1977.

298. Lucas, James. *War in the Desert*. 1st American edition. New York: Beaufort Books, 1983.

299. Lucas, Laddie. *Malta: The Thorn in Rommel's Side: Six Months That Turned the War*. Leicester, England: Ulverscroft, 1992.

300. Luck, Hans von. "The End in North Africa." *MHQ: The Quarterly Journal of Military History* 1, no. 4 (1989): 118-127.

301. Luck, Hans von. *Panzer Commander*. New York: Praeger, 1989.

302. Lyall, Gavin, ed. *The War in the Air: The Royal Air Force in World War II*. New York: William Morrow, 1969.

303. MacCloskey, Monro. *Torch and the Twelfth Air Force*. New York: Richard Rosen Press, 1971.

304. MacIntyre, Donald. *The Battle for the Mediterranean*. New York: W. W. Norton, 1964.

305. MacKenzie, Compton. *Eastern Epic, Volume One, September 1939-March 1943, Defence*. London: Chatto and Windus, 1951.

306. Macksey, Kenneth. *Afrika Korps*. New York: Ballantine Books, 1968.

307. Macksey, Kenneth. *Beda Fomm*. London: Pan Books, 1971.

308. Macksey, Kenneth. *Crucible of Power: The Fight for Tunisia 1942-1943.* London: Hutchinson, 1969.

309. Macksey, Kenneth. *Kesselring: The Making of the Luftwaffe.* New York: David McKay, 1978.

310. Macksey, Kenneth. *Rommel: Battles and Campaigns.* New York: Mayflower, 1979.

311. Macmillan, Harold. *The Blast of War, 1939-1945.* New York: Harper and Row, 1968.

312. Majdalany, Fred. *The Battle of El Alamein: Fortress in the Sand.* New York: J. B. Lippincott, 1965.

313. Majumdar, S. K. "Auchinleck of India in the Middle East (1941-42)." *Journal of the United Service Institute of India* 101, no. 425 (1971): 327-347.

314. Makar, Ragai N. *Egypt.* Santa Barbara, Ca., 1988

315. Marey, Georges. "Field Marshal Montgomery," *Review Militaire Generale* 8 (1972): 178-193.

316. Mars, Alastair. *British Submarines at War 1939-1945.* London: William Kimber, 1971.

317. Marshall, Howard P. *Over to Tunis: The Complete Story of the North African Campaign.* London: Eyre & Spottiswoode, 1943.

318. Mason, David. *Who's Who in World War II.* Boston: Little, Brown, 1978.

319. Matloff, Maurice and E. M. Snell. *Strategic Planning for Coalition Warfare.* 2 vols. Washington, DC: Department of the Army, 1953-59.

320. Maugham, Robin, *North African Notebook.* London:Chapman & Hall, 1948.

321. Maughan, Barton. *Australians in the War: Tobruk and El Alamein.* Canberra: Australian War Memorial, 1966.

322. Maule, Henry. *Out of the Sand: The Epic Story of General Leclerc and the Fighting Free French.* London: Odhams, 1966.

323. Maule, Henry. *Spearhead General: The Epic Story of General Sir Frank Messervy and His Men in Eritrea, North Africa and Burma.* London: Oldhams Press, 1961.

324. Mayer, S. L. and W. J. Koenig. *The Two World Wars: A Guide to Manuscript Collections in the United Kingdom.* London, 1976.

325. McBride, Barrie St. Claire. *Farouk of Egypt: A Biography.* London: Hale, 1967.

326. McMatton, Timothy L. *Operational Principles: The Operational Art of Erwin Rommel and Bernard Montgomery.* Ft. Leavenworth: U.S. Army Command and General Staff College, 1985.

327. Meese, Giovanni. *Come Fini La Guerra in Africa: La "Prima Armata" Italiana in Tunisia.* Milan: Rizzoli, 1946.

328. Mejcher, Helmut J. F. "North Africa in the Strategy and Politics of the Axis Powers, 1936-1943," *Cahiers de Tunisie* 29, no. 3-4 (1981): 629-648.

329. Menzies, Sir Robert Gordon. *Afternoon Light.* Melbourne: Cassell, 1967.

330. Messenger, Charles. *The Tunisian Campaign.* London: Ian Allan, 1982.

331. Micallef, Joseph. *When Malta Stood Alone (1940-1943).* Malta: Interprint, 1981.

332. Millet, Allan R. and Williamson Murray, eds. *Militry Effectiveness.* Vol 3, *The Second World War.* Boston: Allen and Unwin, 1988.

333. Milligan, Spike. *"Rommel?"--Gunner Who?": A Confrontation in the Desert.* London: Book Club, 1975.

334. Mitcham, Samuel W., Jr. *Triumphant Fox: Erwin Rommel and the Rise of the Afrika Korps.* New York: Stein and Day, 1984.

335. Mittelman, Joseph B. *Eight Stars to Victory: A History of the Veteran Ninth U. S. Infantry Division.* Columbus, OH: 9th Infantry Division Association, 1948.

336. Montgomery, Bernard Law. *El Alamein to the River Sangro.* London: Dutton, 1948.

337. Montgomery, Bernard Law. *The Memoirs of Field-Marshal the Viscount Montgomery of Alamein, K.G.* New York: Da Capa Press, 1982.

338. Moore, J. H. *Morshead--A Biography of Lieutenant-General Sir Leslie Morshead.* Sydney: Haldane, 1976.

339. Moorehead, Alan. *African Trilogy.* London: Hamish Hamilton, 1944.

340. Moorehead, Alan. *Montgomery, A Biography.* London: H. Hamilton, 1947.

341. Moorehead, Alan. *Montgomery.* Newport Beach, CA: Books on Tape, 1988 (Cassettes of book).

342. Mordal, Jacques. *Bir Hakeim.* Paris: Presse Pickett, 1970.

343. Morgan, Kay Summersby. *Eisenhower Was My Boss.* New York: Prentice-Hall, 1948.

344. Morison, Samuel Eliot. *Operations in North African Waters October 1942-June 1943. History of United States Naval Operations in World War II.* Vol. II. Boston: Little, Brown, 1950.

345. Mortensen, Daniel R. *A Pattern for Joint-Operations: World War II Close Air Support, North Africa.* Washington, DC: Historical Analysis Services, 1987.

346. Mosley, Leonard. *The Cat and the Mice.* London: Arthur Barker, 1958.

347. Murphy, Robert. *Diplomat Among Warriors.* Garden City, NY: Doubleday, 1964.

348. Murphy, W. E. *Relief of Tobruk.* Official History of New Zealand in the Second World War. Wellington: R. E. Owen Government Printer,1961.

349. Murray, Williamson. "Review of David Fraser's *Knight's Cross,*" *The Journal of Military History* 59, no. 2 (April 1995): 345-46.

350. Nehring, Walter. *Die deutsche Panzerwaffe, 1916-45.* Berlin: Propyl_en, 1969.

351. Neillands, Robin. *The Desert Rats: 7th Armoured Division, 1940-1945.* London: Weidenfeld & Nicolson, 1991.

352. Newton, Don, and A. Cecil Hampshire. *Taranto.* London: William Kimber, 1969.

353. Nicolson, Nigel. *The Life of Field Marshal Earl Alexander of Tunis.* New York: Atheneum, 1973.

354. Nofi, A. A. "The Desert Fox: Rommel's Campaign for North Africa, April 1941-December 1942," *Strategy and Tactics* 87 (1981): 4-15.

355. O'Neill, Herbert C. *The Tide Turns: The Battles of Stalingrad, Alamein, and Tunisia.* (23 Aug. 1942-14 May 1943). London: Faber & Faber, 1944.

356. Oliver, R. Leslie. *Malta at Bay.* London: Hutchinson, 1942.

357. Oliver, R. Leslie. *Malta Besieged.* London: Hutchinson, 1943.

358. Orange, Vincent. *Coningham: A Biography of Air Marshal Sir Arthur Coningham.* London: Methuen, 1990.

359. Orpen, Neil. *Salute the Sappers.* Johannesburg: Sappers Assoc., 1981.

360. Orpen, Neil. *War in the Desert.* Cape Town: Purnell, 1972.

361. Overy, Richard. "Doubts about Rommel," *Times Literary Supplement,* December 10, 1993.

362. Owen, Roderic. *The Desert Air Force.* Foreword by Lord Tedder. New York: Hutchinson, 1948.

363. Pack, Stanley W. C. *Cunningham the Commander.* London: Batsford, 1974.

364. Pack, Stanley W. C. *The Battle of Matapan.* London: Batsford, 1961.

365. Pack, Stanley W. C. *The Battle of Sirte.* Annapolis, MD: USNIP, 1975.

366. Pappas, George S. *United States Army Unit Histories.* Carlisle Barracks, Pa., 1971

367. Parkinson, C. Northcote. *Always a Fusilier.* London: Sampson Low, 1949.

368. Parkinson, Roger. *The Auk: Auchinleck, Victor at Alamein.* New York: Granada Publications, 1977.

369. Patton, General George S. *War As I Knew It.* New York: W. H. Allen, 1950.

370. Paxton, Robert O. *Vichy France: Old Guard and New Order, 1940-1944.* New York: Alfred A. Knopf, 1972.

371. Peniakoff, Lieutenant-Colonel Vladimir. *Private Army.* London: Cape, 1950.

372. Perlmutter, Amos. "Military Incompetence and Failure: A Historical, Comparative and Analytical Evaluation, " *Journal of Strategic Studies* 1 (1978): 121-38.

373. Perowne, Steward. *The Siege Within the Walls: Malta 1940-1943*. London: Hodder and Stoughton, 1970.

374. Pfannes, Charles E. and Victor A. Salomone. *The Great Commanders of World War II*. 4 vols. New York: Zebra, 1981-82.

375. Phillips, Cecil Ernest Lucas. *Alamein*. Boston: Little, Brown, 1962.

376. Phillips, Lt. Col. H. G. "The Aftermath: One Participant's Story," *Army*. Vol. 43, No. 2, Feb. 1993, 42-43.

377. Pitt, Barrie and Frances Pitt. *The Month-by-Month Atlas of World War II*. New York: Summit Books, 1989.

378. Pitt, Barrie. *Churchill and His Generals*. London: Sidgwick & Jackson, 1981.

379. Pitt, Barrie. *The Crucible of War: Western Desert 1941*. London: Jonathan Cape, 1980.

380. Pitt, Barrie. *The Crucible of War: Year of Alamein 1942*. London: Jonathan Cape, 1981.

381. Pitt, Barrie. "Tobruk," *British Heritage* 3, no. 2 (1982): 38-51; no. 4: 36-47.

382. Playfair, Ian Stanley Ord. *The Mediterranean and the Middle East*. Vol. 1. *The Early Successes Against Italy (to May 1941)*; Vol. 2, *The Germans Come to the Help of Their Ally (1941)*; Vol. 3, *British Fortunes Reach Their Lowest (September 1941 to September 1942)*; Vol. 4: *The Destruction of the Axis Forces in Africa*. London: Her Majesty's Stationary Office, 1954-1988.

383. Pogue, Forrest C. *George C. Marshall: Ordeal and Hope, 1939-1942*. New York: Viking Press, 1966.

384. Pogue, Forrest C. *George C. Marshall: Organizer of Victory, 1943-1945*. New York: Viking Press, 1973.

385. Pollock, A. M. *Pienaar of Alamein: The Life Story of a Great South African Soldier*. Cape Town: Cape Times, 1943.

386. Poolman, Kenneth. *Night Strike from Malta: 830 Squadron, R.. N. & Rommel's Convoys*. London: James, 1980.

387. Puleston, W. D. *The Influence of Sea Power in World War II*. New Haven, CT: Yale University Press, 1947.

388. Raeder, Grand Admiral Erich. *My Life.* Annapolis: U.S. Naval Institute, 1960.

389. Rame, David [Arthur Durham Divine]. *Road to Tunis.* New York: Macmillan, 1944.

390. Ramsey, Guy. *One Continent Redeemed.* Garden City, NY: Doubleday, 1943.

391. Rasor, Eugene L. *British Naval History Since 1815: A Guide to the Literature.* New York, 1990

392. Raugh, Harold E., Jr. *Wavell in the Middle East, 1939-1941: A Study in Generalship.* New York: Brassey's, 1993.

393. Ray, Cyril. *Algiers to Austria.* London: Eyre & Spottiswoode, 1952.

394. Reed, Rowena. "Central Mediterranean Sea Control and the North African Compaigns, 1940-1942," *Naval War College Review.* 32, No. 4 (1984): 82-96.

395. Reuth, Ralf. *Des Füehrers General.* Munich: Piper, 1987.

396. Richards, Denis and H. Saunders. *The Royal Air Force.* Vols I and II. London: HMSO, 1954.

397. Richards, Denis. *Portal of Hungerford.* New York: Holmes & Meier, 1990.

398. Richardson, Charles. *Flashback.* London: Kimber, 1985.

399. Richler, Mordecai, ed. *Writers on World War II: An Anthology.* London: Chatto and Windus, 1991.

400. Ritchie, Lewis. *The Epic of Malta.* London: Oldhams Press, 1964.

401. Roach, Peter. *The 8:15 to War: Memoirs of a Desert Rat: El Alamein, Wadi Halfa, Tunis, Salerno, Garigliano, Normandy, and Holland.* London: Cooper, 1982.

402. Roberts, G. P. B. *From the Desert to the Baltic.* London: Kimber, 1987.

403. Rollins, Peter. "Document and Drama in Desert Victory," *Film and History* 4, no. 2 (1974): 11-13.

404. *Rommel, Erwin. Field Marshal of the German Army.* BBC-TV and Time-Life Films. New York: Time-Life Multimedia, 1976.

405. *Rommel vs. Montgomery.* Motion Picture. David L. Wolper Production.

Wilmette, IL: Films Incorporated, 1964.

406. Roskill, Stephen W. *A Merchant Fleet in War.* London: William Collins, 1962.

407. Roskill, Stephen W. *The War at Sea, 1939-1945.* Vol. 1, *The Defensive.* Vol. 2 *The Period of Balance.* London: Her Majesty's Stationery Office, 1956.

408. Ruge, Friedrich. "The Trail of the Fox: A Comment," *Military Affairs*, XLIII (October 1979): 158.

409. Sadat, Anwar. *Revolt on the Nile.* London: Allan Wingate, 1957.

410. Sadkovich, James J. ed. *Reevaluating Major Naval Combatants of World War II.* Westport, CT: Greenwood Press, 1990

411. Sadkovich, James J. "Re-evaluating Who Won the Italo-British Naval Conflict, 1940-2," *European History Quarterly* 18, no. 4 (Oct. 1988): 455-71.

412. Sadkovich, James J. *The Italian Navy in World War II.* Westport, CT: Greenwood Press, 1993.

413. Sainsbury, Keith. *Churchill and Roosevelt at War.* New York: New York University Press, 1994.

414. Sainsbury, Keith. *North African Landings, 1942: A Strategic Decision.* London: Davis-Poynter, 1976.

415. Salewski, Michael. *Die deutsche Seekriegsleitung, 1935-1945.* Franffurt am Mein: Bernard und Graefe, 1970-73.

416. Schmidt, Heinz Werner. *With Rommel in the Desert.* London: G. G. Harrap, 1951.

417. Schoenbrun, David. *Maguis: Soldiers of the Night: The Story of the French Resistance.* London: Robert Hale, 1990.

418. Schofield, B. B. *The Attack on Taranto.* Annapolis, MD; U. S. Naval Institute, 1973.

419. Schreiber, Gerhard, Bernd Stegemann and Detlef Vogel. *Das Deutsche Reich und Der Zweite Weltkrieg. Band 3: Der Mittelmeerraum und Sudosteuropa.* Stuttgart: Deutsche Verlags - Anstalt, 1984.

420. Scoullar, J. L., *Battle for Egypt: The Summer of 1942.* Wellington: Department of Internal Affairs, 1955.

The War in North Africa

421. Sears, Stephen W. *Desert War in North Africa*. New York: Harper & Row, 1967.

422. Shankland, Peter and Anthony Hunter. *Malta Convoy*. New York, Washburn, 1961.

423. Shaw, Kennedy. *Long Range Desert Group*. London: Collins, 1945.

424. Shores, Christoher F., Brian Cull and Nocol Malizia. *Malta: The Hurricane Years, 1940-41*. Carrollton, TX: Squadron Signal Publications, 1987.

425. Shores, Christopher and Hans Ring. *Fighters Over the Desert: The Air Battles in the Western Desert June 1940 to December 1942*. New York: Arco, 1969.

426. Shores, Christopher F. *Malta: The Spitfire Year, 1942*. London: Grub, 1991.

427. Sibley, Rober and Michael Fry. *Rommel*. New York: Random House, 1974.

428. Sixsmith, Eric Keir Gilborne. *British Generalship in the Twentieth Century*. London: Arms & Armour Press, 1970.

429. Slessor, John Cotesworth. *The Central Blue: The Autobiography of Sir John Slessor, Marshal of the RAF*. London: Cassell, 1956.

430. Smeeton, Miles. *A Change of Jungles*. London: Hart-Davis, 1962.

431. Smith Jr., Myron J. *Air War Biblilography, 1939-1945 English Language Sources. Vol. I: The European Theater*.

432. Smith Jr., Myron J. *World War II at Sea: A Bibliography of Sources in English. Vol. I: The European Theater*. 1976.

433. Smith, Myron J. Jr. *World War II: The European and Mediterranean Theaters. An Annotated Bibliography*. New York, 1984.

434. Smith, Peter Charles. *Massacre at Tobruk:The Story of Operation Agreement*. London: Kimber, 1987.

435. Smith, Peter Charles. *Pedestal:The Malta Convoy of August, 1942*. London: Kimber, 1970.

436. Smithers, A. J. *Rude Mechanicals*. London: Leo Cooper, 1978.

437. Smyth, John. *In This Sign Conquer: The Story of the Army Chaplains*. London: Mowbray, 1968.

438. Spivak, Marcel and Armand Leoni. *La Campagne De Tunisie, 1942-1943*. Paris: Service Historique De L'Armee De Terre, 1985.

439. St. Clair McBride, Barrie. *Farouk of Egypt: A Biography*. New York: A. S. Barnes, 1968.

440. Stead, Gordon W. *A Leaf Upon the Sea: A Small Ship in the Mediterranean, 1941-1943*. Vancouver: University of British Columbia Press, 1988.

441. Steiger, Rudolf. *Armour Tactics in the Second World War: Panzer Army Campaigns of 1939-41 in German War Diaries*. New York: Berg, 1991.

442. Stein, M. L. *Under Fire. The Story of American War Correspondents*. New York: Julian Messner, 1968.

443. Stevens, G. R. *Fourth Indian Division*. Toronto: McLaren, 1948.

444. Stevens, W. G. *Bardia to Enfidaville*. Wellington: Department of Internal Affairs, 1962.

445. Stewart, Charles F. *The Ninth Evac: Experiences in a World War II Tent Hospital in North Africa and Europe*. New York: Vantage Press, 1990.

446. Stewart, Richard A. "Rommel's Secret Weapon: Signals Intelligence," *Marine Corps Gazette* 74, no. 3 (1990): 51-55.

447. Stock, James W. *Tobruk: The Siege*. New York: Ballantine Books, 1973.

448. Stone, Brian. *Prisoner from Alamein*. London: H. F & G. Witherby, 1944

449. Strawson, John. *El Alamein: Desert Victory*. London: Dent, 1981.

450. Strawson, John. *The Battle for North Africa*. New York: Scribners, 1969.

451. Strobridge, Truman R. "Old Blood and Guts and the Desert Fox," *Military Review* 64, no. 6 (1984): 33-48.

452. Stussman, Morton J. *Follow Thru*. Stuttgart: Scheufelle, 1945.

453. Sweet, John J. T. *Iron Arm: The Mechanization of Mussolini's Army, 1930-1940*. Westport, CT: Greenwood Press, 1980.

454. Swinson, Arthur. *The Raiders: Desert Strike Force*. New York: Ballantine Books, 1968.

455. Taylor, A. J. P. *English History 1914-1945*. New York: Oxford University Press, 1965.

456. Taylor, A. J. P. *The Second World War: An Illusrated History*. New York: Putnam, 1975.

457. Taylor, Philip, ed., *Britain and the Cinema in the Second World War*. London: Allen and Unwin, 1975.

458. Taylor, R. J. *Kiwis in the Desert: The North African Campaign, 1940-1943*. Wellington: New Zealand Military Studies Centre, 1992.

459. Tedder, Arthur. *With Prejudice: The War Memoirs of Marshal of the Royal Air Force Lord Tedder*. Boston: Little, Brown, 1966.

460. Templer, C. R. "Guns Against Tanks: The Battle of Medenine, March 1943," *Army Quarterly and Defence Journal* 117, no. 1 (1987): 80-83.

461. Terraine, John. *The Right of the Line: The Royal Air Force in the European War, 1939-1945*. London: Hodder and Stoughton, 1985.

462. Thomas, R. C. W. *The Battles of Alam Halfa and El Alamein*. London: Clower, 1952.

463. Thompson, R. W. *Churchill and the Montgomery Myth*. New York: M. Evans, 1968.

464. Thompson, R. W. *The Montgomery Legend*. London: Allen and Unwin, 1967.

465. Thruelsen, Richard. *Mediterranean Sweep: Air Stories from El Alamein to Rome*. New York: Duell, Sloan & Pearce, 1944.

466. Tooley, Robert William. *Montgomery As Military Trainer: Preparation for Alamein*. M.A. Thesis, University of New Brunswick, 1984. Ottawa: National Library of Canada, 1986.

467. Trevor-Roper, H. R. *Hitler's War Directives 1939-1945*. London: Sidgwick & Jackson, 1964.

468. Truscott, Lucian K., Jr. *Command Missions*. New York: E. P. Dutton, 1954.

469. Tuker, Francis. *Approach to Battle*. London: Cassell, 1963.

470. Tunney, Christopher. *A Biographical Dictionary of World War II*. New York: St. Martin's Press, 1972.

471. U. S. Coast Guard. *The Coast Guard at War*. Vol. IX: *North African Landings*. Washington, DC: U. S. Government Printing Office, 1946.

472. Ufficio Storico della Marina Militare. *L'organizzazione della marina il conflitto*. (Rome, 1972).

473. Ufficio Storico della Marina Militare. *Le Azioni navali im Mediterraneo dal 10 Giugno 1940 al 31 Marzo 1940*. (Rome, 1970).

474. Van Creveld, Martin. "Rommel's Supply Problem, 1941-42," *Journal of the Royal United Services Institute for Defence Studies* 119, no. 3 (1974): 67-73.

475. Van Creveld, Martin. *Supplying War: Logistics from Wallenstein to Patton*. New York: Cambridge University Press, 1977.

476. Verney, Gerald L. *The Desert Rats*. London: Hutchinson, 1954.

477. Verrier, Anthony. *Assassination in Algiers: Churchill, Roosevelt, deGaulle, and the Murder of Admiral Darlan*. London: Macmillan, 1990.

478. Von Mellenthin, F. W. *Panzer Battles, 1939-45*. London: Cassell, 1955.

479. Von Taysen, Adalbert. *Tobruk 1941: der Kampf in Nordafrika*. Freibourg: Verlag Rombach, 1979.

480. Walker, David A. "Oss and Operation Torch," *Journal of Contemporary History* 22, no. 4 (1987): 667-679 (Based on Hoover Institution Archives).

481. Walker, Ronald. *Alam Halfa and Alamein*. Official History of New Zealand in the Second World War, 1939-45. Wellington, N.Z., 1967.

482. Warlimont, General Walter. *Inside Hitler's Headquarters*. London: Weidenfeld & Nicolson, 1962.

483. Warner, Oliver. *Cunningham of Hyndhope: Admiral of the Fleet*. London: John Murray, 1967.

484. Wedemeyer, Albert C. *Wedemeyer Reports!* New York: Henry Holt, 1958.

485. Weigley, Russell F. "Shaping the American Army of World War II: Mobility versus Power," in Lloyd J. Matthews and Dale E. Brown, *The Parameters of War:*

Military History from the Journal of the U. S. Army War College. New York: Pergamon-Brassey's, 1987.

486. Weigley, Russell F. *The American Way of War: A History of United States Military Strategy and Policy.* Bloomington: Indiana University Press, 1977.

487. Weinberg, Gerhard L. *A World at Arms: a Global History of World War II.* New York: Cambridge University Press, 1994.

488. Wellard, James. *The Man in a Helmet.* London: Eyre & Spottiswoode, 1947.

489. Westphal, General Siegfried. "Notes on the campaign in North Africa, 1941-1943," *J. Royal United Service Inst* 105, no. 617: 70-81.

490. Westphal, General Siegfried. *The German Army in the West.* London: Cassell, 1951.

491. Wheal, Elizabaeth-Anne, Stephen Pope, and James Taylor. *A Dictionary of the Second World War.* New York: Peter Bedrick Books, 1990.

492. Whiting, Charles. *Kasserine: The Battlefield Slaughter of American Troops by Rommel's Afrika Korps.* New York: Stein and Day, 1986.

493. Willison, Brigadier Arthur C. *The Relief of Tobruk: A Tribute to the British Soldier.* Luton, England: Leagrave Press, 1942.

494. Wilmot, Chester. *Tobruk, 1941: Capture, Siege, relief.* Sydney: Angus and Robertson, 1944.

495. Wolfert, Michael L. *From ACTS to COBRA: Evolution of Close Air Doctrine in World War Two.* Maxwell AFB, AL: Air Cmd. & Staff College, Air Univ. 1988.

496. Woolcombre, R. *The Campaigns of Lord Wavell 1939-1943.* London: Cassell, 1959.

497. Wordell, M. T. and Seiler, E. N. *"Wildcats" Over Casablanca.* Boston: Little, Brown, 1943.

498. Yarborough, William P. *Bail Out Over North Africa: America's First Combat Parachute Missions, 1942.* Williamstown, NJ: Phillips, 1979.

499. Yindrich, Jan. *Fortress Tobruk.* London: Benn, 1951.

500. Young, Desmond. *Rommel: The Desert Fox.* New York: Harper, 1950.

501. Young, Peter. *Atlas of the Second World War.* New York, 1974.

502. Zanuck, Darryl F. *Tunis Expedition.* New York: Random House, 1943.

503. Ziegler, Janet. *World War II: Books in English, 1945-1965.* Stanford, CA, 1971.

504. Zuckerman, Solly, *From Apes to Warlords.* New York: Harper & Row, 1978.

Index

About the Author

COLIN F. BAXTER is professor of history at East Tennessee State University. He also compiled *The Normandy Campaign, 1944: A Selected Bibliography* (Greenwood, 1992) and is the coeditor of *The American Military Tradition from Colonial Times to the Present* (1993).

www.ingramcontent.com/pod-product-compliance
Lightning Source LLC
Chambersburg PA
CBHW020359100426

42812CB00001B/120